WE STAND
OUR GROUND

To Bondi
from Hirnio Hahn
dec. '88

WE STAND OUR GROUND

THREE WOMEN, THEIR VISION, THEIR POEMS.

KIMIKO HAHN • GALE JACKSON
SUSAN SHERMAN

ArtWork by Josely Carvalho

NEW YORK, NY

MARGARET RANDALL'S poem, "Blood Loosens Its Stranglehold," appeared in *CONDITIONS: FOURTEEN*, 1987. Reprinted by permission.

Certain of these poems have appeared previously in the following publications to whom grateful acknowledgement is here made:

GALE JACKSON: *Art Against Apartheid: Works for Freedom, Black American Literature Forum, IKON, Minnesota Review*

KIMIKO HAHN: *Bomb, Conditions, Contact II, IKON, 'Jes 'Grew, Poetry Project Newsletter, The World*

SUSAN SHERMAN: *Amazon Poetry, Art Against Apartheid: Works for Freedom, Giants Play Well in the Drizzle.... Heresies, IKON, Lesbian Poetry, LibeRATion, Mulch, Number, Sinister Wisdom, 13th Moon, Waterways: Poetry in the Mainstream, With Anger/With Love, Women Poems Love Poems*

Cover design by Ann Cammett
Cover type by George W. Romaka, Classic Composing Inc.
Cover art by Josely Carvalho
Special thanks to Janet Newell
Printed in the United States by McNaughton & Gunn, Inc.

First Edition, First Printing

Library of Congress Cataloging-in-Publication Data
Hahn, Kimiko, 1955–
    We stand our ground.

    1. American poetry--Women authors. 2. American
poetry--20th century. 3. Women and literature--
United States. I. Jackson, Gale, 1958-   .
II. Sherman, Susan. III. Title.
PS589.H34 1988   811'.54'0809287   88-3020
ISBN 0-945368-01-1
ISBN 0-945368-00-3 (pbk.)

IKON Inc. P.O. Box 1355, Stuyvesant Station, New York, N.Y. 10009

All these years beyond placebos filling our mouths, slivers
of glass and sand tearing our feet
we knew beyond mixed messages and no messages
beyond heavy rules and doors closed
by others and also by ourselves.

The face that said no the arms that said no the grace
of god or patriarch.
We understood and the island dried our tears.
We stood our ground.
We stand our ground.

Margaret Randall
Albuquerque, Summer 1986

CONTENTS:

CONVERSATIONS/CORRESPONDENCE

POEMS
Kimiko Hahn

Gale Jackson

CONTENTS:

Susan Sherman

Three Voices Together: A Collage

Kimiko Hahn, Gale Jackson, Susan Sherman

(The following excerpts were edited from a series of letters, discussions and taped conversations that took place from July through October, 1987)

"My work is informed by where I am from..."

Kimiko Hahn: Some of my earliest memories rise from my family's visit to Maui to see my (maternal) grandparents. I was four and very confused about nationality, about being "American." (I'm half Japanese-American; my mother's from Hawaii, and half German-American, my dad's from Milwaukee.) Children called me Chinese or Japanese — physically, I look Asian. Could I be Japanese and American? Part Japanese?

I remember asking my grandmother if she were Japanese. She laughed and said, "Yes." Then she asked me. I replied, "A little bit." I remember being confused and being asked a lot: "What are you?" Now people ask, "Where are you from?"

When I was nine we lived in Japan while my father studied art. The children in my Japanese school called me "amerikajin" or "gaijin" (literally, "outsider"). I felt I never fit in. I never felt fully "at home." My poems address this ambiguity, for example, in "Instead of Speech" or "Her First Language."

Growing up in a white middle-class suburb in effect polarized my identity. I grew away from the Western tradition in a sense (except for poetry and rock-and-roll). I was raised with a lot of Japanese culture mainly because of my father's deep interest and my mother's heritage; my sister and I studied flower arrangement, classical and folk dance, calligraphy, tea ceremony. In college then graduate school I went on to study Japanese literature, seeking both the familiar and the new. Something that felt comfortable. In the poem, "Revolutions," I open with the little-known fact that the "golden age of literature" was dominated by women in Japan. This influence of theirs happened for social reasons because the men were writing in Chinese (the same as people wrote in Latin instead of in the vernacular) whereas the women were writing in the vernacular in Japanese. So the women's writing was an explosion; it was a release of material and feelings — so much so men would write in the female persona. The "female sensibility" was that dominant. To me this is a very important piece of history and part of myself. It inspires and informs much of my own art.

9

Parallel to this was my political "awakening," beginning with a feminist orientation. I sold copies of the original newsprint booklet of *Our Bodies, Our Selves* in high school. When "caught" I retreated to a nearby parking lot where the girls picked up their orders. My own sexuality became a territory for me: my body is mine, my responsibility. This "territory" also gave me an increasing awareness that women's bodies historically have not always belonged to them; for instance, fathers using their daughters as marital pawns or husbands using wives to produce sons.

It is strange that while I do not consider my ideology "Feminist" (capital F) in the sense of men or patriarchy being the enemy, all my work is deeply committed to women's relationships (with one another, with men, with society). This is especially true of the poems I've collected here. In "Seizure," I view revolution not as a "midwife" but as birth itself. "Revolutions" is more or less about a female culture or aesthetic. "Seams" was commissioned by Bill Brand for his experimental film (*Coalfields*) on Black Lung advocate Fred Carter — my particular subjective contribution (I was also interviewed and helped edit) takes a "feminist position," envisioning the strip-mined land as "female" and reaching for the kind of power (sexual and social) the word "virile" engenders. I think my longer poems further explore a female sub-culture: "Resistance" through the metaphor of weaving (traditional women's work); "Poetic Closure" through the metaphor of closure/divorce. It may be simplistic to say "but" because women have been unencouraged and unpublished for centuries, what we say today is new and exhilarating. Our work and concerns are very different from men's and it has something to do with biology (the powerful, mysterious and vulnerable uterus) and a lot to do with history. I'm not knocking male writers, rather expressing my particular need for other women's voices.

Gale Jackson: I am a Black woman. An African American woman. My mother's first child. My grandmother's fourth, but first American born. Older sibling. The one who writes. My great aunt's special. And sometimes "patti g."

On my mother's side my people are African Carribbeans from Jamaica, the West Indies. Their continuous immigrations (I've never thought of my people's immigration as a static concept) allowed me to understand internationalism at an early age. I heard I took my first plane ride at age six months and my great grandmother, who I knew as a child, was a great traveler as well--up thru the island nations, thru South and Central America, as one did working in the colonized world of that day. My father's side of the family are African Americans who have been in this country longer, I suspect. The truth is that I don't really know.

I grew up in a very large household (very African I've learned, very West Indian also) with several generations and family groups and special names and relationships to everyone. I have always lived with older people and new born babies belonging to a community with a measure of security and a measure of rule. We were not particularly rich or poor, but I am, have always been, clear that our well-being as individuals was absolutely tied into our helping each other along. This is the axis of my politics. This is what we were told and what we saw done. I grew up with cousins and lived in the same household as great grandmother, grandmother, uncles and aunts. My mother always worked. The older women, at different times, kept house. We were taught (maybe the saving naivete of immigrant children) that we could create the life that we would.

I grew up in a home of women who were smart, independent and self-sufficient. These are the things you learn by osmosis. I am sure that I am among many writers of similar background who attribute their love of stories to their early delight in listening to the women talk. The women in my house gossiped, talked music. Talked politics. Talked sports. They spoke several languages. They have, as Jamaicans, a dual concept of home. (They don't pronounce the "h" but they say home and mean Jamaica even here while they live in the psychic space that they've created in this country which they also call, in a way, home.) To imitate not only their storytelling but also the language of their stories was always a special game for me as a child. I remember longing to be grown so I would have stories to tell and a language of my own.

I come from a place where there is a lot of love and respect. I feel gifted and responsible. Having been socialized to share and to see myself as a part of a community — my family and by extension my people and then by extension our world — leaves you with tremendous strength and the real responsibility to carry on. To take it further. To put something back. Like a new place. New words. New possibilities for home.

My work is informed by where I am from; my Africas in America, my Caribbean journeys, loving myself, women, children, (smile) even how I love the men. I want the work to be loving portraits, reminders to people of their strength, stories to extend the imagination about where we can go. Like in "the untitled" which begins with my friend's grandmother, Mrs. King, a woman who is an emotional and physical axis for her family. The poem begins with this real Black woman at its heart, then takes you to Central America and her women, to South Africa and the real women there, back to Brooklyn, back and forth until it is one place, a place where we can begin to imagine what will happen when she has had enough and decides to 'soar,' change the world, take it out. Possibilities. The language to tell. The language to see with and be empowered by enough to reach on out and connect. In a language that is our own.

Susan Sherman: I like the word "origins" because to me it means not only your childhood or your roots (your starting point in time) but what continues, what makes your work, your daily life possible. In "Ten Years After" there's a line, "…what we move toward is what moves us most." My origin: what moves me, touches me; what moves me, activates me, defines me, most.

I was born in Philadelphia, Pennsylvania in 1939, grew up in Los Angeles during the 40s and 50s. My memories of my family are attached to those years. When I finished college in 1961 I came to New York and didn't return to California for over 17 years.

Berkeley in the late 50s and early 60s — the Beat Generation, the San Francisco Renaissance, North Beach, poetry, the "sexual revolution" and my first real experiences with sex and love — unfortunately then not the same; my first relationship with a woman, the House Un-American Activities Committee "riots;" the first time I saw a real alternative to the life I had known or the lives I knew about, an alternative I wanted to embrace.

New York, 1961, '62, '63, poetry readings at the *Deux Megots, Le Metro,* writing and directing plays at the *Hardware Poets Theatre,* working for $28 a week, apartments on Delancy and Suffolk, on 9th St. between B & C, the riots in '63, '64, the episodes of disassociation, panic, not seeing my family for years. The struggle to survive. The mid 60s — *Angry Arts Against the War, the Free University, the Alternate University,* the founding of the first series of *IKON,* "coming out" in 1961 and then slowly retreating in and then "coming out" again. The trips to Cuba in 1967 and 68 — and consciousness of a reality totally separate from any I had recognized before — loss of job, ulcer, loss of magazine, turning that loss into intense political involvement and commitment and creativity, not born from, but energized by anger — as my poetry had been, from personal anger, from a consciousness of my parents' brutality, years before.

The 70s — Chile, breakup of first long relationship, the 5th St. Women's Building, the Lesbian/feminist movement, the stillness of years that were a pulling together as well as a breaking apart; *Sagaris,* a bad automobile accident. The 80s — Nicaragua, the new *IKON,* a new relationship. All that I remember, all I have forgotten. My origins, what made me, make me what I am.

To talk about all this with any completeness would take a book in itself — being close to fifty, a half century now. And I'm actually in the process of writing that book. More than anything else to try to get some of the feeling of those years down, not "my" years, the years themselves. So much of them, as so much of our own individual histories, forgotten or distorted.

My childhood was characterized by a lack of roots, of specific place. I never knew exactly where my grandparents were from, my parents never spoke of it, if they knew themselves. Partly from fear, partly because they wanted desperately to forget those years, to fit in. I am Jewish, and that was thought of then in racial, not religious terms. I wasn't brought up in the Jewish religion, I went to a Christian Science school (I left Christian Science when I was 15) although we celebrated most of the important Jewish holidays at home and I was often the only one who went to synagogue with my father on high holidays, and I was always very aware of being Jewish and of a proud and troubled heritage.

It was only long afterwards, when I learned about words like "background"and "class" that I realized how important my parents' immigrant experience was in explaining a lot of what happened to me in my early life. And the importance of understanding that experience now. The multiplicity of cultures and the constant pitting of those cultures against each other. The multiplicity of centuries — in a place like New York, in the space of a few square blocks. And the incredible problems and the incredible energy and creativity which that produces.

Our class definitions were confused — my mother was the only child in her family born in this country, my stepfather (who raised me) came here from Russia at the age of five — he never went past grammar school. My mother hated poverty; I think there was a certain grayness attached to her childhood memories, to being poor, that became a kind of metaphor for her. It wasn't until I got much older that I realized how many of her choices were conditioned by that hatred. She moved as far away from her family as she could get. So I never had "family" around when I was growing up. I remember only once visiting my grandparents when I was quite young. I remember them being nice to me — they didn't speak English so I couldn't understand what they said — and that their apartment smelled of crackers and warm milk.

"The Fourth Wall," written around 1964, was the first time I really tried to deal directly with any of these issues in my poems.

As I get older, the hardest part seems to be able to continue defining myself in terms of my hopes, my dreams, my vision — to keep identifying and re-identifying myself with what I believe, what I think is human and just. And, perhaps most important, to allow myself to risk being wrong. In my writing as well as in my life.

"Breaking through towards expression..."

Gale: I write because I am compelled to, by circumstance, by desire. I write like I could scream sometimes. Or sing. Compelled by love to mark the moment. Compelled by pain.

Writing is like living. It is absolutely intimate and absolutely social. It is something that is personally felt even while it is resonant with many voices. Conscience. Haunting. It's that close. The world around you is insistent and specific and real and you have to put it down. You have to say something about how we are living. About life. To say. To shape. To explore. With words. With voice. To celebrate. To mourn. To recreate.

The kids out in the street can be so shouting, so wildly alive. While in our silences we are dying a little each day with AIDS, famine, the death squads who invade. You write to tell the stories that need telling. Of course that is political. Our culture is our social heart. Our histories. Our possibilities. Our names. How we survive whole. This is about how a woman moves thru the world alone. This is about Nicaragua's sovereignty. About Palestine's homeland. About South Africa's freedom. About hunger. About home. You write to tell the stories that need telling. You hear it and it matters. You nurture the imagination of voice as it rises up.... A scream, a note, a song, a shout, a silence, a cry.... Making way in the world.

Kimiko: It was a real need for other voices, like yours and Susan's, that thrust me into poetry. Writing for me is the process of breaking through towards expression and finding time to write is important to my well being. My poem "Going Inside to Write" is based on a real woman whose place of privacy was the bathroom. Her desperation for expression lead her to write there. I feel for her.

When I look back at my childhood, although we were a family of artists and were close in mutual activities, we did not express our emotions to each other. I vividly recall my mother and father telling me to put on a cheerful face in spite of whatever I was feeling, then turning to my friends and encouraging them to express themselves. In high school it became heightened when my father would tell me my "bad moods" ruined his day. My parents assumed my sullenness was an adolescent stage.

Susan: It wasn't an easy thing to speak in my family either. Often when really emotional about something, I would start to stutter — not a noticeable stutter to anyone, more like a hesitation, an inability to force the words out, to find the right ones. I feel my writing expresses that deep part of me. It takes the language of the poem, the images of the poem — reaching beyond words — to do it.

From the time I was very young reading was my refuge, but I never read poetry. The poems I had contact with were typical grade school and high school poems, written in another century, in another language, having nothing to do with me. The poems I wrote when I was a teenager were about my own life, my own dreams, written in my own language, unsure and poor as it was.

It was when I was in Berkeley in 1958 and met Diane Wakoski and all the poets there that poetry came alive for me. It was about me, my generation, my hopes, and in my language. As I read those poems, and often mimicked their gestures, my own language in writing changed, and my own voice began, slowly, to emerge.

Gale: Someone once said "Art is like a lover" because it is the job of art to show you, like a lover can show you, the things that you can't see. The things that are there that are not yet seen. There are ways of sharing vision. Art. Of caring. I remember once finding my mother's drawings in a sewing stool, in those years when I was very young and making books and selling them to her for nickels and encouragement. She is a very fine artist. Realistic. Drawing portraits. Concerned with the lines. The feelings in the human face. Tho she no longer draws, she has created that kind of a household. Around her. So full. And the cozy and wide-angled world view which begins with the intense importance of each individual face.

Kimiko: I was just thinking about what it means to be an artist right now in this environment. I was thinking that it's so much like working a second shift — second shift, third shift whatever. You work, you come home and the day begins again doing your true work; it's a continual tradeoff and compromise.

My life works best when everything is integrated — making money, politics, my art, my relationships. Everything is really intertwined. But when did that ever happen! I can only think of one time — when I worked on *Coalfields*. The two poems "Seams" and "Coalfields" are from that film. I traveled with Bill Brand in West Virginia, conducted, then excerpted interviews. I didn't promise him poems because I usually don't write on assignment like that, but I said I'd write some text and I wrote these two poems I really like — I think they're probably my best. They're political, they're sexy, they're forceful.

For ten days we did nothing but talk to active miners, retired miners, their wives, their kids in some cases and heard extraordinary stories. I'd return to my motel room exhausted, but type away, and that's where these poems originated. The whole experience integrated what I love, what I feel passionate about — that is so rare and it just needn't be. Why should we always think of ourselves as having to scrape around for moments to do our artwork! (And being a mother now means even less time.)

Susan: We're trying to do our art now as women who have to work to survive. As women who can't depend on anyone else to support us. Who are self-supporting. Well, this is obviously nothing new. This is the reason women, people of color, working people, have always been so under-represented in the art world, not because of a lack of talent, because they have lacked both the time to do the work and the places to publish or show their work.

Gale: There are a lot of myths about what and where art is. On this side of the "arts" spectrum there are women, people, the majority of the world who, it's true, have not had the establishment forums, but who have always had art in their own lives and it's own (even when it has been very confined) spheres. For most of us maintaining our cultural identity has been a crucial, political act. I think that is one of the things Kimiko's "Resistance" poem talks about. There has always been a people's art. It may have been quiltmaking to tell the story of family generations, jewelry, craft that identified a particular people, or pictures cut from magazines and pasted up to give color to a wall. At our best we create a living art. Today we are, again, saying that we want to take the best of that tradition and imagination, particularly as women, and exercise it in the widest international spheres. We are saying to take the art, the beauty, the understanding and the values that have informed our lives and insured our survival, what we've used to make a home, to make a just and better society.

I feel very utilitarian about art. I look at what the traditional functions of art have been — they've been about education and comfort, about being in harmony with the world and getting dreams out. Art is a vehicle not just for beauty, but for all the possibilities of things people have inside. Folktales, for example, teach people, remind them of the rules of their society, kindle their imaginations, their concept of possibility and of reach. Storytelling, like quiltmaking, brings people together with a vehicle of expression within the context of what they must do. Within the context of their society and its work. It is at best an interaction, a progress in the world that is interactive, not self-destructive.

I always think of the Innuit people and the storytelling they do thru the dark days, because it's freezing cold and this is a part of the tradition they have created to sustain themselves and be in harmony with their environment. Well, in this country, in this city, the question is, how do you bring that here, to this wild urban place?

Connections are very important for me. I feel that my strength as a writer grows with my ability to tap into my cultural traditions. From knowing who I am. Being an African American woman, for instance, in this time is an extraordinary moment in history that I am a part of. Understanding that allows me to move in and out in powerful ways. It allows me to connect with other women from a very strong place. It allows me a very international understanding of myself in my time. My political work is for me the logical extension of my understanding and my concern, in the same way that my writing combines caring and craft to move towards broader understandings, visions.

From the time I was thirteen, I knew that I lived in an absolutely interdependent world economy. this is a real challenge to the human imagination. My mother couldn't say that, my mother didn't wear socks from Afghanistan or have an idea of what was happening in Afghanistan and see it on television. There is a balance, a tension, a consciousness between the particular (the one loved one, the family, the self) and the international (the universal, the world). Within that tension somewhere is where I live and write.

Kimiko: I write from a very unconscious place. When I write I sit down with a blank piece of paper and I just scribble. Whatever comes up, that's what I shape and re-write and work over. Vision and revision! There are occasions when I have something I have to write about, but what I do is store the idea until it becomes part of that place I write from. We all self-censor to a greater or lesser degree, but my most successful poems are the ones that spring from that unself-conscious place.

Susan: In every poem I have ever written I am looking for meaning. Not "How?" — which is a series of physical causes, but "Why?" This is what the poem "Facts" is all about. We have been taught not to ask, "Why?" With the result that we wind up in the dilemma of my student in the poem, unable to understand even the most obvious truth, what's right in front of us.

I find my inspiration, as far as form is concerned, first of all in music — which is one of the things I love most. It is the rhythm of the poem, the music of the voice that captures me. And then with imagery — to make the statement precise and unusual. And simple. The complexity of the simple, of the simple statement. I'm not telling stories in most of my poems; I'm not describing events. If anything, I'm painting states of mind, composing themes, trying to come up with new perceptions, new ways of relating what I observe around me — like the old way philosophy was written, in poetry — but adding our new consciousness, our personal and social life and the events that take place around us.

I understand how philosophy got and continues to get "bad press," but I'm not talking about a kind of intellectualism that plays with language or abstract concepts and refuses to be grounded in any kind of real social context. Behind everything we do and say is an assumption, and one of the things philosophy is about to me is understanding and questioning those assumptions.

With Anger/With Love was an appropriate name for my first full book. Love is an obvious connection, but the anger is not anger that ties you to the hated object; it is anger that energizes you to *change* that condition.

"Political involvement is not an abstract thing..."

Kimiko: While no one escaped the influence of the Vietnam War, I was not a conscious voice in the Movement (say in the '60s to early '70s). When I did venture towards Asian American organizations (which is to say an organized struggle) there was a little animosity: being part white translated to part enemy. Back then.

Not until I lived in New York and began to feel oppressed by the economic and social environment did I begin to understand my own personal dilemma: female, non-white, artist, member of the working class. My boyfriend said to me, "Well, what are you going to do about (your anxiety and anger)?" As a step toward comprehension and vision I began to study Marxism-Leninism. For the first time I cared about the study of history and political economy and through those studies I began to think in an analytical manner quite different from what I had encountered in college. A scientific manner. I began to appreciate science and to learn I could use my mind to understand current world events. However, this was the early '70s, a time when sectarianism was rampant, and the Left was isolated from "the working class."

But my real cultural and political work did not take off until Oct. '81 at the *American Writers Congress,* a gathering of over 3,000 writers in New York. I found myself in the midst of political people who had trained in every place you find writers: from trade union newsletter editors from steel and auto plants to university professors to street poets. We were there to talk politics. Dissent. Make resolutions. (The most concrete product, or by-product, was the *National Writers Union.*) I was in my element though still young in the sense of being politically "fresh." At this time I met more Asian American writers and having completed a stint in graduate school, I was aching to quit the libraries, to write and organize. My activity began with my editorship at *Bridge: Asian American Perspectives* (now defunct).

After a few years of projects, projections and a couple of trips to Nicaragua (where I met Susan), I was invited to help form the Poets and Writers Committee of *Artists Call Against U.S. Intervention in Central America.* This would be my next "leap forward." I met other writers/ political activists and began to hone my organizing skills. Being on the Steering Committee gave me a chance to exercise my political views which were to keep *Artists Call* on track as an organization against intervention (and undeniably pro-Sandinista). The organization faded away after a couple of years for a variety of personal (many original organizers started families) and political reasons. Political? In my opinion we should have linked the issue of intervention (the bloated military budget, for example) with our real needs here. Artists' needs are not separate: we need food, housing, medical care, schools for our children. Part of the reason we (and most of society) don't have adequate social services is because so much is taken up by the military. I consider illiteracy, unemployment and homelessness our real national security risks. I wish we could have made these links, brought the issue of intervention closer to our own needs, rather than conveniently keeping it one of "the poor Central Americans." We cannot afford to be sectarian any longer: our allies, say, in shelters for the homeless here, may not even know what socialism is. They may never have heard the word "proletariat," but if they are struggling against this economic system, we must become allies.

Gale: One favorite writer friend says, "be subversive" — she talks in the poem "deepwater." Subversive be much of the crux of it. Inadvertently. At first. I found that this imagination would be the only way for me to making a living and write and care.

When I began my work with *Art Against Apartheid* I was working as a Black Heritage librarian. Doing a lot of cultural programming. Telling stories. Helping to build the collection in a very special community-run space — the *Langston Hughes Community Library and Cultural Center*. He had always been my first poet. A working artist.

Five years before that I had been standing at Grand Army Plaza in Brooklyn trying to figure out what I could do here where I lived. It was the museum. The park. Or the library. So library it turned out. I had, still have, these biographies for children I wanted to do. I been in and out. Doing some free-lance research. Uncovering. Discovering. In Black women's history. In myself. The concept of the bookarts, story-arts, and the politics of information.

Much before that were lots of beginnings. Some anti-nuclear work in college, some coming together with other Black students. In a women's space. Around then was when I began to do research and writing for community based organizations. I worked with the *War Resisters League*. Some extraordinary people who had been around, militantly for peace, more than twice the time of my life. Learning about finding and disseminating information in organized "alternative" structures. The educational work for justice. Had many important apprenticeships. In writing. In organizing as well. I grew up to be a librarian thru alternating between these special works and some of the regular jobs women find themselves doing at one time or another. All these things forced my eye. The political work. The craft. The shit work. I went naturally into the work with children and it has stretched me out in all possible directions. To teach. To perform. To program and organize in the arts. To be faster and more smart.

I keep being a librarian in different settings. Now at Medgar Evers College, a predominately Black women's college in Brooklyn, pushing the status quo out — I feel like I'm still building. Being a juggler. But no more than the women before me who got me to this spot. To that multi-generational coalition I must attribute (smile) the strength of imagination for survival.

Susan: It has always seemed to me that the greatest weapon that can be and is used against us is isolation. Separating us from one another. What depresses me most, inactivates me most is when I feel that I'm totally and completely alone, in my work as well as in my relationships. That I have no community.

I'm not talking about the physical event of being a single entity in a room. You can be in a room with a thousand people and still feel alone. I first heard this conceptualized in the 60s when I was teaching at the Free University — or School as it came later to be known because of legal restrictions — a place where I felt I was really able to share what I knew and at the same time learn from people who were gathered together there to learn and teach for the purpose of directly influencing and changing the world they lived in. Or rather the worlds. Since we came from many different places. Where information was used instead of stored, where, at its best, there really was dialogue, a willingness, an eagerness to participate, to talk and to listen. To break down the artifical and imposed separation between words and action, poetry and real people's lives.

At many crucial points in my life, from childhood on, I have seen and experienced forcefully and often quite painfully the results of isolation and lack of community, not only on myself but on people around me. That's why it's been so important to me to make connections. To edit a magazine that makes connections. To do this book.

Kimiko: My political involvement has profoundly influenced my writing. In the same way relationships (romantic relationships, my relationship with my mother, my father, my sister) influence my writing. I think it's given it a totally new dimension and I don't feel at all "agitpropy," like I'm writing something that's for a placard or that, in fact, I can only write one way. I feel very much that there's a new dimension added to my writing that makes it much more powerful. And yes, it means *not* being separated.

Gale: Your politics really mean the configurations of your relationships. We live in a world together and that is a political construct. How we choose to live, our collective imagination about how we can live and what we can do is so tied to our culture. Our culture is after all our eyes. My eyes allow me to see, to have relationships with folks close and far, all my relationships, with my family, my love, my friends, with even the women far away. All that feeds into who I am, my political being. I am in Brooklyn, I can imagine what it must be like to live in a house where soldiers are standing on the roof, with guns. This all my world. I write from here about that voice, about the place where it joins my own. The world is very much with me. Sometimes so much it is difficult to write. But always so important, so urgent, that it brings me back to a place where I have to. You care. You want. A safe place. It is a politic of the deepest desire. We are always saying something about the connections that we forge with one another. We are at best saying something about human possibility for humanity, for a particular articulated beauty, for change. Politically, culturally, it is my job to provide the information about what, how much life means.

Susan: Political involvement is not an abstract thing. You write about it the way you'd write about anything else you have a deep commitment to. It's very fashionable now to argue that American writers are free of the necessity to include political or social issues in our work because those necessities don't impinge on our very existence the way they might in another country like, for example, El Salvador. The implication, of course, being that not only are political issues not an "authentic" part of our existence, they shouldn't be central in "real" art, and that, in this country, one must finally chose between being an artist or an activist. That being an "true" artist automatically means putting issues of "language" first and "society" second.

Of course, this not only ignores the actual day-to-day struggle for survival of a huge segment of the American population, it conveniently excuses from responsibility the very group of people who are directly or indirectly the source of the problems that necessitate activisim to begin with. My question, and I think it's crucial, to those writers, artists, intellectuals would have to be this: Even if your own individual life isn't threatened at this particular instant, at what point do you decide what's being done to other people is worth involving in your writing, your world, at what point do you take responsibility for it, at what point do you suddenly discover that it *is* your world, your responsibility, your work. Whether it's apartheid in South Africa, brutality in the Israeli-occupied territories, or poverty and racism here in the United States.

The real danger, it seems to me, when you become politically involved is not in your choice of subject matter, but how to keep from being overly self-censoring. Maybe it's partly generational, but when I first became involved politically in the middle 60s, I started asking myself questions like, "Should I write about this subject?" "Should I change these words?" I went back through my essays and changed all the masculine pronouns that referred to humanity as "man." And I think that was absolutely right. But it can be carried too far. There was an internalized part of me constantly saying: Is this revolutionary? Is this correct?

And it did affect on my work and did inhibit me for awhile. I'm trying to write about my family now and I feel a lot of conflict and a lot of difficulty trying to be careful, trying to be fair, trying to be political, in the face of an anti-Semitism I acknowledge I cannot possibly understand. After all, I was a child raised in the 40's when the fear of what was happening in Europe and the prejudice and danger that engendered here was an undercurrent that ran through my parents' everyday existence. Fears that were passed on to me in much more subtle ways: The obsession with, whenever possible, passing, assimilating. The contradiction of, at the same time, building a wall around you of your own people, your own customs, traditions, of excluding the life-threatening "other." The fear that falling out of line, being pointed out, being too obvious, would affect not only you, but your family, your whole people. That an individual act could be lethal to the community as a whole.

Gale: How do you be all the things that you are? How can we all be? How can a commitment to humanity be maintained? As we struggle to survive, as we fight wars between and among ourselves. There are a lot of things we have yet to learn. But there has to be something in the deepest voice that you trust and that is the place where you write from. There is something in there that as a cultural worker you are constantly in the process of teaching and learning. We live in a very complicated time. And this is one of the big challenges before us — teaching ourselves to relisten, to be human, to liberate our hearts. I have to believe that is possible. That we have whatever tools we need in our histories. In our stories. There are some very harsh realities. Believing doesn't make me anguish free. But it makes that contradiction, that anguish, that isolation a little different, a little less.

I was talking to somebody about relationships and they were saying, you know, look at the world we live in. We live in a fucking insane world. You want to read the paper, you know what I mean. How do you think that you make it through loving someone else, anybody, how do you think that you get through that scot-free and perfectly and you're always a good person. That none of your society gets into you. But, of course, it does. Into all of us. Women. Men. The children.

Susan: A child has no alternatives. A child's world is proscribed by the adults in it. They define that world. I wrote once the most important thing you can discover is that there is an alternative. And later I learned that if there isn't one, you have to fight to create one. Because that's what being an adult, being in control means. We are kept in the position of children by being deprived of choice.

My trip to the Cuban Cultural conference in 1968 taught me about the history of my own country, because it placed me in a context outside myself, separate from me or the interests of people around me. Because it taught me about revolution, about change and about how art, how culture was part of that process. Because I met writers from Argentina and Chile and Mexico and Columbia and the rest of Latin America, many of whom I had seen in *El Corno Emplumado* (the bi-lingual magazine co-edited by Margaret Randall in Mexico in the 60s), possibly the only place in this country those works were available then, but had never really understood as part of my own culture, my own hemisphere.

In the 50s, with the Beat Movement, poetry really moved out "into the streets" and became a dialogue you spoke out loud, that people listened to and responded too — the readings in the Northbeach bars in the 50's and the open readings in the early 60s in cafes and bars in New York.

The Black civil rights movement and liberation movements, the women's movement, Lesbian and gay struggle, Chicano, Puerto-Rican, Native American, Asian American movements, produced the energy that has motivated and empowered all people to creatively express themselves, to demand their work be recognized and that those artists and activists and thinkers and human beings that form their culture, their "origins" be published, be heard. As progressive Jewish groups had done earlier and now again, and the Irish, and all other groups that came before and will come after carrying on in a long tradition of struggle and change.

And the base of American culture *has* changed, because the way was opened for a new underpinning of culture that was truly representative of the United States as it is today, for all of us, a United States no longer grounded exclusively in European art and criticism.

I'm not talking about stealing someone else's ideas or work, as so often happens in popular music. I'm talking about the fact that we now have so much access to what is truly ours. All the wonderful work that is now available from our America, as well as writers like Gabriel García Márquez and Luisa Valenzuela and Isabel Allende and Pablo Neruda from Latin American and Sembene Ousmane from Senegal and Fumiko Enchi from Japan. They are there for us to absorb the way I read Rainer Maria Rilke and Garcia Lorca in college until they became part of me, part of my history, my own voice, and they were important, but it was a limited history, a European history, and a limited voice, and now it's not, it's an "American" heritage which is all of us in close contact with our own hemisphere, with Central America and the Caribbean and South America and Mexico and Canada too.

I think making a dichotomy between art and politics is part of that whole process of continuing to separate us, of silencing us — which is what the poem "From Nicaragua a Gift" is all about.

I think that it's very important and that people who are involved politically keep saying it, that what we're fighting for is not a world that's smaller than the world we live in. If it gets any smaller none of us are going to be able to breathe at all. What we're fighting for is a world that's larger, where all people can express themselves, where they can express their differences. Where *we* can express *our* differences.

"I say 'poet' now…"

Kimiko: I think when one talks about politics and art, history and memory are essential elements. One is not entirely subjective, the other objective. I think women's history in general is most important to me. I identify with the collective difficulty to express and/or publish that expression. (In fact, this book will be one avenue against that historical silence.) Of course the stereotypical Japanese woman is a passive, silent one. I defy that. I use history and memory to defy it.

The history of the artist in general is one of margins. We are part of the intelligentsia and therefore, in times of social turmoil, we can throw our lot in any direction. We don't have set allies. The social margin we occupy is one that denies us full participation as citizens (especially in being able to make a living) and does not take our occupation seriously. I used to be hesitant to tell people I was a poet. I'd say "writer" or "student." That sounds legitimate. But to admit to being an artist (even though I grew up in a family of artists!) was somehow saying I was not to be taken seriously. I say "poet" now.

Politically I do my organizing with artists because I don't think real social change is possible without cultural change — that's where artists come in — yes, even poets! Who reads and listens to poetry? I read in a variety of places and that's where people mainly hear me. And a great many people write all over this land — I mean there are a lot of poets out there. Nicaragua is called "A Land of Poets" because you can go anywhere and find them. Well, I think that is true here though our society doesn't value poets/artists as highly. Just look at the proliferation of journals, newsletters and workshops. What I'd like to do politically is say to these writers — your lot is really cast with all working people, therefore, everyone from meat packers in Minnesota to welfare mothers in Atlanta is our social ally.

What is really the opposite of repression? Usually we think of the opposite of repression as being liberation, but a major part of liberation is expression. Expression empowers people towards liberation, or within a liberation movement, or the liberation of one's heart, or whatever. I was thinking of expression as being perhaps the true opposite of repression. I was thinking of it in a social way.

I grew up in a very white suburb where my sister and I and my mother were the minority. And later on, when I started getting involved with people who were in the Asian-American struggles, some people would look at me as being part white and they somewhat rejected me. Later on it was okay — never mind that in the detention camps during

World War II, if you were some fraction Japanese you were in the camps. I consider my daughter Japanese-American, because if it came to having to go into the camps that's where she would be. I don't know what she'll consider herself, that is for her to decide and for her to live out. But I consider her Japanese-American.

My husband's mother, when we announced our engagement, turned to him right at the dinner table and said--why don't you marry an American? What she meant was white, but what she said was American. American means white, anglo-saxon, protestant. Probably not even Catholic or Jewish. If I'd been Jewish, she would have said something somewhat different, but with the same meaning.

Susan: The truth is when it comes to the bottom line the society you live in always tries to enforce its definitions of who you are on you. And even more important what you mean and what *value* you have. Sometimes fatally. Which is why it's so essential to make our own definitions and to struggle to change social definitions.

Gale: We're talking about human education here. That's when you talk about seizing traditional forms, the arts, traditional forms of reaching people and turning them modern and figuring out how to teach these lessons again because somehow people have watched too many commercials not realizing that culturally, or thru the lack thereof, we've been pushed to the brink of survival, against the wall literally to the edge of the fatal possibilities of the world we're living in. Somehow you have to reach people and bring them back mindful that peace will only come with justice. That eye for eye for eye could go on and on. Somehow you have to reach people 'cause we have to talk. There are a lot of things that, for starters, we need to learn and remember. A lot of history has been taken away from people and one of the first retributions would be to begin to restore. People's very stories have been taken away, made inaccessible, till we don't all know who we are. Culturally. Till we don't have no home. Real or metaphor. Then there is all that is going on that is not being told. The news. Our country's not-so-covert wars. In my work as a writer, as a librarian, I be finding that people don't know. This tragedy of repetition. When it becomes clear that culture, art information, is first and foremost political, it is clear that people need to use that to reach and teach. To explore. People need to know. To imagine. To know.

Kimiko: You've touched on something really important. I keep speaking as if the artists are over here and the oppressed people are over there and we're going to meet, but in fact the majority of artists are part of the survival movement. I can find the time to write because I'm fortunate enough to have a rent-stabilized apartment. But that's part luck and part living in a place for ten years through drug wars and everything else — sticking it out. But the fact is there are people out there who may not consider themselves "poets" but actually are. There are groupings of homeless poets' workshops. Several groupings. So they're already out there working together. It's a matter of seeing our interests as one and the same.

Susan: When I was in Berkeley in 1959, there were the "artists" and there were the "political" people. I was an artist and I didn't consider myself one of the "politicos," although I fancied myself terribly anti-establishment. We slept together, we ate together, we went to parties together, but there was a very distinct separation.

When I went to the demonstration against HUAC after the demonstrators had been washed down a flight of marble stairs in San Francisco in 1960, when I went to anti-war demonstrations after coming to New York, I still considered myself an "artist" — period. I was just protesting certain unjust actions. It was really after my trip to Cuba in 1968 along with the repercussions from that trip (loss of job, the magazine, friends) that I became much more conscious politically, that I began to make connections — to connect the poverty that I suddenly "saw," the racism, the commercialism and recognize their inter-relations, to examine their cause.

At the same time I started to identify myself as an artist who was also a political person and recognize where those two things came together. It was a huge change for me, as big as the one I went through when I first went to Berkeley. And that I would go through later as a result of feminism.

My recognition of myself consciously as a "woman" rather than a being who somehow magically transcended such mundane categories as gender came through the "5th St. Women's Building Action," which took place in coalition with the squatters' movement in the early 70's. I'll never forget that night — standing precisely at midnight in the middle of a snow storm on New Year's Eve, on the corner of 1st Ave. and 5th St. guarding a van full of provisions as women crawled, one by one, each holding a flashlight, into a broken window on the first floor of this huge abandoned building almost directly across from the 9th Precinct. We intended the building to be used by community women — for day-care, for the homeless, for community activities. And it was — at least until we were busted by the Tactical Police Force and it was demolished to make way for a parking lot. It was always my feeling with the level of energy we women showed, they didn't dare leave that building standing.

One of main organizers of that action was June Arnold, the head of the Literature Committee of the *Women's Center,* a feminist author who started one of the first women's presses — in fact, it might have been *the* first — *Daughters Inc.* Our slogan was "Our hands, our minds, our feet, our bodies are tools of change."

"Lilith" was a direct result of that 5th Street action and the months of organizing and "consciousness-raising" that went along with it. I call it my "coming-out" poem — that expression to be taken on a number of levels. It is also a strong statement of support for the many brave woman who had put themselves on the line in the 60s for what they believed in, some of whom were in prison or underground at the time, and additionally, a connection with the late 50s and early 60s, living as a poet on the periphery of society.

Kimiko: What we're talking about really is culture. You can change laws and you can change institutions but culture is something that continues from one state to the next and you can't say — "Smash it" like you can a building or an institution or a structure. It is, like history, something that continues.

My feeling is that there are social motions right now that are not your conventional political motions, for example, it may be more like homelessness, undocumented workers. We have to look at things that are happening and not expect to see the same things. Again, that's where the artist as a visionary and as a creative person really plays an important role, because we don't always look for things as they're supposed to appear.

Gale: I think of a lot of the stories of Black women writers, and myself included, who really trace the beginning of their writing to people telling stories, to women telling stories, or the kitchen, you know. But that's a reality for so many people. That's an underground culture. A subversive survival culture. The same kind of thing that was somehow able to come in Japan, that certainly nurtured the story telling instinct of so many writers today. So many Black women writers now. From a place that people understand. The trickle down theory clearly doesn't work in economics, in politics, or culture or anything else. You have to figure out how much is here from a language that people all speak, from a language that gets defined as you speak it. This movement, for life, for peace and social justice must tap into creating a way for people to be empowered. To write the scenario for their own lives. We want to claim the power for people to really name themselves and to make some decisions about how to live.

You know, there's some kind of meeting in-between what people who have learned to move people and work with people, i.e. political people, and people who have learned to move people and work with people, i.e. artist people — there's some meeting of their knowledge that's absolutely necessary, that's an even exchange here. And that needs to be recognized as that. And both sides suffer from that lack of recognition.

If you don't liberate peoples' hearts, you pass the civil rights bill one more time. And again and again and again. The problems we face demand the fullest of our capabilities. Our imagination. Anger. For example, picture yourself in this city, how do people find new structures for dealing with what our lives are? Once you get to the core — somebody doesn't have a home, what do people do then? That takes incredible imagination. These are the places that organizing and imagination absolutely must meet.

Kimiko: This doesn't mean that we have to write only about those issues in order to ally ourselves with them. I read at a demonstration put on by the National Union of the Homeless — homeless people who organized themselves — and I read mainly love poems. The context was like this: if a husband or wife or whoever are in a shelter, now how are they ever going to have any intimacy? You know, if you don't have a home, you don't have a home life. I wanted to read love poems in that context.

People of color, poor people, are being blamed for pulling down the standard of living and for the violence in our society when in fact it's the fault of the system itself that creates these conditions, exploits people and victimizes them. There's a different way to lynch people these days. You just let them be homeless, or you shoot them in the back and get away with it. I think the way artists can work against this is through political clarity, through understanding what's going on and trying to use their voice, because artists have a platform that other people don't have. Again, not that we have to write poems about any particular subject — if people want to that's fine — but you can also get up and say a word on your platform and then do what you gotta do, sing a song, or play a flute or whatever. But I think clarity is what's important.

Gale: Which happens within groups of people, groups of people learning about themselves in the way you learn about yourself from the inside out and at the same time between people looking at each other and learning something else about themselves by learning something else about somebody else. And that kind of process being able to happen, which assumes the absence of fear. And in this society that's a big assumption.

Susan: You know, that really brings up our relationship to each other. This kind of book that we're doing doesn't come out of nowhere. It's the continuation of a process rather than the beginning of one. And part of it is that I felt I could sit down with you and not be afraid to talk about anything. That we trust each other because we've known each other for a long time — we've worked together and respect each other.

Kimiko and I met at the Conference on Central America in Managua, Nicaragua in 1983, we worked together on the original organization of *Ventana* — a cultural support group for the ASTC (Sandinista Cultural Workers Association) and in connection with *Artist's Call.* Although I published a poem of Gale's in the second issue of *IKON*, we didn't actually get to know each other until *IKON* organized a benefit poetry reading for *Art Against Apartheid,* a coalition of artists and arts' organizations.

Gale: That was in 1984 when we were initiating a major drive to inform and agitate people on the anti-apartheid front as well as drawing the domestic issues connections. Then *AAA* and *IKON*, Gale and Susan came together again to edit an anthology, *Works for Freedom,* of anti-apartheid work; a collection of over one hundred artists work.... Now me and Kimiko we met in Blue Mountain doing some strategic planning (smile) for artist response and networking in urgent political times....

I like the concept of collaboration and what it can be when it's good. I think that it's like what musicians do when they jam and create a new moment in music. The trick is to understand the differences in each voice. The different needs. The different tones. And roads that bring us here. Each player brings her own music. One comes for the challenge. One comes to hear the sounds. Another comes out of the need to move with others. You kinda cup your ear. Like a good singer. Pick up your beat. Your key. Your notes. Then I guess it's like jumprope: there's a moment then the downbeat opens up and you can slide in in stride. One voice after another gets in there. Best if they all be distinct. But you get a new music. Familiar and different in the end.

KIMIKO HAHN

The Bath: August 6, 1945

Bathing the summer night
off my arms and breasts
I heard a plane
overhead *I heard*
the door rattle
froze
then relaxed
in the cool water
one more moment
one private moment
before waking the children
and mother-in-law,
before the heat
before the midday heat
drenched my spirits again.
I had wanted
to also relax
in thoughts of my husband
when he was drafted
imprisoned — but didn't dare
and rose from the tub,
dried off lightly
and slipped on cotton work pants.
Caution drew me to the window
and there an enormous blossom of fire
a hand changed my life
and made the world shiver —
a light that tore flesh
so it slipped off limbs,
swelled so
no one could recognize
a mother or child
a hand that tore the door open
pushed me on the floor
ripped me up —
I will never have children again
so even today
my hair has not grown back
my teeth still shards
and one eye blind
and it would be easy,
satisfying somehow
to write it off as history

those men are there
each time I close
my one good eye
each time or lay blame
on men or militarists
the children cry out
in my sleep
where they still live
for the sake of a night's rest.
But it isn't air raids
simply
that we survive
but *gold worth its weight*
in blood the coal,
oil, uranium we mine
and drill
yet cannot call our own.
And it would be gratifying
to be called a survivor
I am a survivor
since I live if I didn't wonder
about survival today —
at 55, widowed at 18—
if I didn't feel
the same oppressive August heat
auto parts in South Africa,
Mexico, Alabama,
and shiver not from memory
or terror
but anger that this wounded body
must stand *take a stand*
and cry out
as only a new born baby can cry—
I live, I will live
I will to live
in spite of history
to make history
in my vision of peace—
that morning in the bath
so calm
so much my right
though I cannot return to that moment
I bring these words to you
hoping to hold you
to hold you
and to take hold.

Seams
(Coalfields Text 1)

The seam was gray as a recollection—
I mean, as that recollection
(even in my motel room)
of the shirts my husband packed in his suitcase,
the toothbrush and razor,
of the door I closed after him
as I said *sorry*—
gray as the morning air
in Dupont City full of Dupont.
That Thursday was my day
to not talk about Fred Carter's case.
And Blue, an unemployed coalminer,
hardly talked
but drove us around
pulling over to pick up coffee
or apples
adjust the windshield wipers
and I felt sadder for the red
than the raw yellow
in the hills. How to take
this virility (yes) in my heart—
the politics
that make my blood surge—
and place it in the feminine land:
the seams, drift mouth,
strip mining, hollars.
So on a steamy autumn day
I could smell
something like Ortho cream or rubber
except it was Dupont
a late Thursday afternoon.
Was it this female
that forced the men to tender moments
(even *art*)
in the shafts
or made me hope Fred into saying
whereas the lungs are like a sponge
even as the company
invades his very alveoli.
If I could be a virile woman
I would be these sorry hills

separate and gorgeous
where the plain language
(black lung)
becomes stripped.
Where the thin-seam miner
guts the side of a mountain.
Where some men cut open some kid's stomach
in the parking lot
for being black with a white girl.
That, too, landscape.
Also, that day — with the coal
pouring out of the tipple —
was so exquisite
I just sat in the car.
Some moments I stopped breathing
as the rain sprayed through the window
across my cheeks and sweater.
Fred would never last a week in jail
and they know it   I knew
I was home
when I mistook mantrip for mantrap.
The men winked and offered
wanna go down?
I smiled: *a couple inches or a few yards*
That made them ask
where you from anyway?
Between sass and conversations with Blue
or how he got his name
when the other miners threw him out of the shower
into the snow — a kind of hazing —
and how he paints while he watches the tv
and the kids
and how I write on the subways —
I knew the extra suitcase
my husband left behind
wouldn't hurt me
everytime I went for my hairbrush.
He'll never come home.
Fred would have a heart attack
in that hole
Miners never die of natural causes
in the lungs of the south —
in Dupont City, Kanawha, Goshen, Confidence,
Left Hand, Five Forks, Clover Lick

(*Coalfields* Texts for a film by Bill Brand, 1984)

Coalfields (text 2)
30 Seconds on Fred Carter

Blue first told me about Fred Carter—
an old black retired miner,
black lung victim, lay representative,
who was up on some misdemeanors.
He said the feds framed him
for being effective
and running for UMW president.
His running mate said
they knew where me and Fred was coming from
and we could organize
every nonunion mine in this country.
His lawyer said
Fred has the most impressive forearms
I ever did see.
And to tell you the truth
I didn't believe much of it
until I saw his three bedrooms
filled with hats and suits.
Files. Suitcases. Cases.
And a second story.

Revolutions

for P

Forbidden to learn Chinese
the women wrote in the language
of their islands
and so Japanese
became the currency of high aesthetics
for centuries
as did the female persona: the pine
the longing. This is the truth.

(We can rise above those needles.)

The red silk from my grandmother
amazes me. Think of the peasant
immigrating from rice fields
to black volcanic soil. The black beaches.
The children black
in this sunlight
against the parents' will or aspirations.

(Anywhere else
girls of mixed marriages would be prostitutes or courtesans.)

I want those words
that gave women de facto power,
those religious evocations: dreams so potent
'she became pregnant' or 'men killed'
or 'the mistress died in pain.'
I connect to that century
as after breath is knocked out
we suck it back in.

The words the men stole after all
to write about a daughter's death
or their own (soft) thigh
belongs to us — to me —
though translation is a border
we look over or into;
sometimes a familiar noise
('elegant confusion'). But can *meaning*
travel
the way capital moves
like oil in the Alaskan pipline

or in tankers in the Straits of Hormuz?
Can those sounds move like that?
Yes. But we don't understand.

But we don't know
what it means to speak freely
even to ourselves. Patricia,
fertility is not the antithesis of virility.
I can't help it.

If I could translate the culture
women cultivate
I would admit to plum
and plumb.

I always begin with a season.
Like: snow and plums in the wooden bowl
make me love him. How
I warm one in my fist
then lick it until the skin
grows so tender it bursts
beneath my breathing.
The yellow is brilliant.
The snow is warm.

Some of our lessons issue from song
because there are never enough
older sisters
especially from the South via Detroit

where we look for a model
with the desperation of a root —

where a bride is a state —

where *heat lightning* is pronounced:
lie down on my breast
so your tongue and teeth reach my tit
and I can —

where yes —

I didn't learn the diction from the Classics
rather transistor radios. Confidence
in my body also. After years —

the confidence that gives and gives
and is not afraid to take either.

Exploring the words means plunging down
not skimming across
or watching whitecaps however lovely.
Not balking at fear either:
the walls are filled with sounds,
the windows, with sorrow.

Revolution for example is the soft
exact
orbit of planet, moon, seed.
Also seizing the means of production
for our class.
Where does that come from?
It all begins with women, she said.

Like the warp and woof of cloth.

And how there's no 'free verse' so we'll search
for the subtle structures: the poetic closure,
the seven kinds of ambiguity, etc.

Not tonight dear.

How it's not so sad really
for a husband or wife
to come alone.

Komachi's reputation came from legend:
the 99th time a lover visited her door
(the night before she would let him enter)
he died.

That's the breaks.

In a patriarchy is such cruelty cruelty
or survival? Is
the father to blame for ugly daughters, too?
for the unruly ones?

Come sit by the radiator and open window.
When the baby hiccoughed inside her
her whole body shook.

After birth is not a time or reform
it belongs to a separation we turn toward.

Her First Language

is not American
so when she recites the poem
the worlds are not as clear
as the beautiful notes
from her mouth.
Teeth figure into not only this section
but recollections of grandpa
and the glass by his bed.
You could cry for his plumeria
and chickens.
The other plantation hands
brought his wife laundry
and stalks of cane.
The T-shirts
glistened on the line.
He couldn't speak to you
though he said *iiko da ne*
and patted you on the head
somehow like the German girl offstage
saying
the moon is writhing.
It occurs to you
only women and wounded soldiers
writhe.

Instead of Speech

The reflection of Noh actors
in the reflecting pool, the torches,
the faces all turned in one direction
make your heart throb:
this is home. This is home the way a home
will never admit you
because you are by definition alien and female.

       No matter what (bitchy, manipulative, fertile,
       on top)
       you girl
       are the vulnerable one by social
       and biological inheritance.
       At the moment.

       All women are streetwise, she said
       and, *the penis is the linchpin
       of linguistic systems.* Funny

       the word penis.

       He recognized the comb as something
       you bought for the honeymoon you didn't take.

       After the separation
       his girlfriend interfered with your grief
       so you wanted to — to what?

The actor's feet never left the ground
as he slowly whirled across the wooden stage
toward anything.

       All summer you wore your husband's gym shorts and T-shirts
       Do you wear that in the street? she asked.
       A man asked the same.

Carpenters construct a stage
so stamping and pounding resound
like the chest cavity.
I'm told ceramic urns are planted beneath
in strategic locations.

On a subway poster of a voluptuous woman
someone drew in tits
and a cock stuck up her ass. *Had it been a man*
there might be a cock stuck in his mouth
not a cunt.
The evermore unattached phallus.

— you wanted to rip her fucking face off —

A woman with short blonde hair and white earrings
entered the cafe.
She wore an immaculate white T-shirt
and you knew were you a lesbian and she were
you would approach her
and court her.

There are only actors
yet so many female roles
so many women's masks it hurts.

I would like to climb the stage
in white tabi and silk
stretch my arms out — fingers together palms down —
and stamp.
Calling out: *nantoka nantoka soro*

      like sorrow, sorrow sorrow

The New Father

for Ted

Setting aside her rattle and doll
you stretch across our bed
and draw me over you.
We curve into each other and pulse gently
until my breasts spot your chest with milk.

Poetic Closure

Affection came easily
like dust or salt spray
or leaving.
Yet it could not have been anywhere.
Curling up in my new studio
I thought of rain and wished it —
to extinguish the outside —
to make the surface of everything blurred.
I was cleaning
and thought how rust feels like his face in the morning
as I leaned against him
or blurred his complexion on a holiday.
But affection for anything came easily as rain —
if it showers now you see him (or me)
now you don't. My reflection
coincided with the lightning
and I knew, like women for centuries,
I am without father or husband
only partly by choice.

The taxes, insurance, bills —
seemed like my whole life.
I could barely think
or fall asleep for days.
Though it's women who comfort
we leave our mothers at birth
for fathers to give us away
in, say, a couple dozen years.
While the boys never leave.

I know if it rains while I sleep
I will rise for the open window
like walking toward a crib.

When I think of looking for an apartment
I think of metal: stainless steel, green copper,
rusted pipes.
And stoops toward early evening
with families fanning themselves

and playing dominoes.
There were lots with grass,
the kind that feels like razors.
A few green or brown bottles,
a Midnight Express.
It was fall.

It was fall when I hurt my mother:
I said it's possible
I may be alone for the rest of my life.
I wondered: childless?
with an old dog and beat-up typewriter?
She changed the topic.
She promised herself to change
against all odds
like the woman in the Tosa Diary
(written by a man)
who had lost her daughter.

"I kept my attention on the beautiful sight ashore, and as the
ship rowed on, the mountains, the sea, all darkened as night
fell. One could not distinguish north from south and could only
entrust the weather to the captain's understanding. Even a man
accustomed to a sea voyage at night must find it disheartening.
For a woman it was worse, nothing to do but hold one's head
against the floor down in the boat and weep aloud. While I was
so dejected, the men of the ship or the captain fell to singing
boat songs til it could scarcely be borne.

>   "In the spring fields I cried aloud in pain—
>   The young pampas grass had cut, had cut my hands;
>   I managed at least to pluck some shoots,
>   And shall I take them to my parents?
>   Will my mother-in-law make them a meal?
>   And how can I get home?"

How would that be, have been, in the year 935
to leave in the provinces a daughter's ashes
and travel by boat to the capital
where her husband would be?
No comfort from concubines or a mother-in-law.

How could I measure this in 1985?

What do you mean what does he want?
do you know what you want?
aside from a daughter like your younger sister:
pliant as grass or wild iris
and clean as clay in a stream.
I could wade in and breathe water
like fish
in the woods there behind the house.
The greatest childhood dangers: poison ivy,
strange men and dinosaurs.

If you push yourself you reach endings
again and again. Right smack in the middle
of a thought or breath
(we're back to breath).

I would love to hold you Ruth
back when you were, say, fourteen,
in 1918
when you were smart and virginal
(I imagine)—
not to kiss your mouth or breasts
but to cry until my body shakes.

Maybe this one will understand:
he brought a flower
though I misunderstood the gift
and ignored it. I'm sorry.
It's a little thing to you — but to me
I'm sorry.
Had I known I would have touched it to my nose
like a puppy
who understands everything thus.

"In societies like the Nuer, bridewealth
can only be converted into brides. In others, bridewealth
can be converted into something else, like political prestige."

"The world of corporate finance is unrelated to the real world
of goods and services. Instead of generating new wealth,
corporations are playing a giant game of asset rearrangement
that is largely unproductive. It's a symptom
of a longer-range economic problem — a fear of the future."

Maybe if I had known Ida
as a woman and not my great-grandmother
maybe I would have liked her for more than fudge
and cloth corsages.
Maybe I would forgive her for not letting father
meet his grandfather.

The Phelps Dodge strike in Morenci, Arizona
began over a year ago
and the striking miners see themselves
as fighting not only the company but the law.
One month after the walk out
with 700 police officers and National Guardsmen on hand
the company reopened the plant. Before the strike
the average wage was $14 an hour;
today the company is paying $10, with new employees receiving $7.

Looking for an apartment was so heart-wrenching
I could only think of her
lying on the bottom of the boat sobbing
as the waves lapped the hold.
Anything she saw — pebbles on the beach,
a piece of candy, a scrap of cloth —
reminded her of her daughter.
How interesting,
not so much to write in a female persona,
but that he chose the dead child to be a girl.
Scholars do not know how autobiographic the diary may be.

I would ask mother to reread the end of the rhinocerous story
again and again: "But the Parsee came down from his palm-tree,
wearing his hat, from which the rays of the sun
were reflected in more-than-oriental splendor, packed up
his cooking stove, and went away in the direction
of Orotavo, Amygdala, the Upland Meadows of Antananarivo,
and the Marshes of Sonoput."

He left the apartment until I found something I could afford.
He had tried to leave before
the difference now was that it was the first time
I didn't try to stop him. Something like mothballs
or turpentine held me back.
Something in my throat.

Marie came home with me that afternoon
and I showed her my sister
playing in her crib
and my mother's wedding shoes
which I had found that weekend.
Marie was such a big girl at eight
and mother so small
that they fit.
I was furious. *They're mother's.*

"Besides greenmail, the new vocabulary in the takeover game
includes two-tiered tender offers, Pac Man,
poison pill defenses, crown jewel options,
golden parachutes and self tenders."

After college I found an office-temp job
and moved in with my fiancée.
It was early fall and the barrio was still hot.
Hawkers sat on the corner with avocados,
platanos and crates of fish.
I was twenty-two and felt this is it.
I'm ready.

"The Phelps Dodge miners live in often bleak surroundings
in the hot, treeless camps on the lips of the mines
and in the shadows of the tall smelter smokestacks.
...If you can break a strike here
you can break a strike anywhere."

      "Always I look back
      Toward my native place,
      To where my parents are,
      And how can I get home?
"His song touched the feelings of us all. As he was singing and
the boat bore on, we passed a place where dark-colored birds were
gathered upon the tops of rocks along the coast, while the waves
scattered white at their base. It was as the captain said: 'The
white waves are heading where the black birds roost.' There was
nothing very special about his words, but at the time they
sounded like the verse of a poem. Since it was not the sort of
thing one would expect a sea captain to say, it caught everyone's
attention."

I thought of Eliot's subtle rhyme, varied and soft,
and the line: "I shall wear white flannel trousers,
          and walk upon the beach."
Then, "I have seen them riding seaward on the waves
Combing the white hair of the waves blown back
When the wind blows the water white and black."

"Mr. Ramsey, stumbling along a passage one dark morning,
stretched his arms out, but Mrs. Ramsey
having died rather suddenly the night before,
his arms though open, remained empty."

If you can break a strike here in Morenci
you can break a strike anywhere. We have a history.

We kept saving each other from despair
and vacationed together:
two young women, fresh and sorrowful.

"[In a poem] the structural principles produce a state
of expectation continuously maintained
and in general we expect the principles to continue operating
as they have operated."

He didn't have an apartment to let
but he thought I would be young like my sister
and easy.
Such scum.

The structure will change like a woman
breaking through a fever
and rising for a glass of water.

I thought of the day my sister was born.
I waved to mother from the hospital parking lot.
Her face looked small
and I got to stay at the Goddard's for the first time.
Meg had just put the constellations on her ceiling
and they glowed in the dark.
I asked daddy if we could go to the Natural History
and get some too.

NOTE: quotations from *Poetic Closure* by Barbara Hernstein Smith, *Japanese Poetic Diaries* by Earl Miner, *The New York Times, To the Lighthouse* by Virginia Woolf, and "The Love Song of J. Alfred Prufrock," by T. S. Eliot.

Toward Strength

For E

Tell me also that the lawns will be covered
with snow even as the flowers
break through.
We think they are delicate
but know their fragrance penetrates the ice.
Or it may be our imagination:
little signals that we'll bear up under hard times
together always.

Going Inside to Write

She finds the only place to write
is the *ote arai*.
So she takes in her notebook
and retells the story of the peach boy:
when the old man and woman
broke open the peach
a dazzlingly handsome baby
with pink cheeks and penis
stepped out and said
chichiue hahaue domo arigato gozaimashita
(thank you).
He was a baby
but he could speak.

In the halflight
she finishes her version.

Here the mind deregulates language.
Outside
causes
are not confined but often conditioned
by an infant's bowel movements,
stacks of dishes,
international economies or classical literature.
Myths and store coupons bear philosophy.

To know the body
from the inside —

the lining of the uterus, the muscles
that squeeze blood out,

the Braxton-Hicks contractions

labor

crisis

c-section —

to know the body from the inside
is warranty against fear

("baby look what you've done to me") —

against the fear

of one's own body,
also toward the possibility of tending oneself
in the onslaught of others.

She will return later
to write about the sparrow
who had her tongue clipped off
for eating the woman's rice starch.

We garden with the knowledge of our bodies.

Though she hears her father
calling from the far room
she shouts:
I can't hear you.
I can't hear you.

Nora

Other women say other women
gave more than Nora
and she says so also.
The streets, named after martyrs,
are filled with women:
Marta, Bertha, Ariel,
Rita, Beatriz, Arlen —
and there are companeras
who can tell you about regiments of men they led
or mothers who joined
in mourning a child's death or rape.
Indeed, Nora spent her Saturdays
at the golf course or poolside
of the country club
outside her father's cattle ranch.
The *adoring* father
pushed this little girl
to a vision broader than sink and bed
in the town then Villa Somoza,
in the days when she dreamed of marrying
someone with an aristocratic name.
But she knew the poor also:
visiting the hospitals crowded as slums
and teaching hygiene and religion
in the slums diseased as the hospitals.
She knew even then charities
would not satisfy.
But when she campaigned
for the opposition leader, Aguero,
her parents sent her to the Catholic University,
Washington, D.C.
and she baked in isolation
from her country's history
and from our own days of massive escalation
and the slaughter of the Vietnamese people
(who would also claim victory in time).
These were, she said, *the two most superficial
years of my life.* 1968
1969
Returning to Managua
Nora entered law school,
believing in justice.

But her lessons revolved around political prisoners
and as my friend, a lawyer, learned,
the law is to *defend*
power and property.
Nora probably felt the same
when a companero approached her;
she began her timid *collaboration*
with the Frente Sandinista de Liberacion Nacional.
Soon she exchanged readings
for meetings and transporting comrades.
Oscar Turcios taught her
within the limitations of her life experiences
until her need was synonymous
with the FSLN —
with the tortured peasants and students
and the exhausted petty bourgeoisie.
Then, too, she met Jorge Jenkins,
student FSLN rep,
and they promised political allegiance first
before their own vows.
She trusted his *higher level*
of political development.
Their engagement caused her father
heart arrest
but she married Jorge.
And slowly, again, she became isolated.
They moved to Italy
where he studied anthropology
and she, banking law and computers.
But isolation is more than geography or class.
I wonder if it was partly morning sickness,
the swollenness beyond expectation,
hunger for everything, anything, nothing —
even at the cost of one's vision.
You need him. You need
to protect the forthcoming —
first one daughter then another.
Or was the isolation *practical*:
when two have a meeting
the woman goes in principle.
But know that the woman
is there bathing the infants,
nursing, singing,
washing rice off the table and dishes
consumed by the house

with little to spare for politics
or oneself.
After five years
of what I've just imagined
Nora divorced her husband;
but, too, she separated from herself.
Was that it Nora?
That queasy sensation
there's nothing under your feet.
So all you can think is
clutch the girls,
become active again or fall.
Meanwhile the number of executions
and disappeared
spread plague-like.
Then it was March, 1978.
Nora, a lawyer for Nicaragua's largest
        construction company,
met General Reynaldo Perez Vega,
the "Dog."
She contacted the compas.
They plotted.
Would she give up everything
(her daughters)
to kidnap him.
But she thought
part of my decision
was precisely because of my children.
So she invited over the General
who'd been waiting for her
to give it up for months.
He arrived within hours
giving her only enough time
to buy some liquor.
But he didn't want a drink
(*what for?* he asked);
he wanted the prize of his patience.
So she began the task:
unbuttoned his jacket,
slipped off his shirt gently
with an urgency akin to passion,
unbuckled his scarred belt,
pulled off his bruise-black boots.
Drawing his pants down

toward her lips
she spoke softly
a signal for her comrades.
They caved into the room like an earthquake
and held him down.
When she went out to tell his bodyguard
go buy us some rum
he couldn't hear the General's calls
above his car radio.
She returned to her bedroom
to find his throat slashed.
The "Dog" fought so intensely
there was no choice.
And it was *just as well*
she thought later
training in the mountains on the Northern Front.
She wondered at what he would have done to her,
had done to many women
when promises weren't hot as a piece of ass
or when that wasn't it.
One less CIA agent, eh Nora?
By June she was ready for combat
and became political leader
of four squadrons on the Southern Front.
Her eldest daughter, then six,
resented her disappearance.
If you had just told me, she said later.
For a mother who belongs to an organization
dedicated and poised to win
what can you say to your daughters.
Do the fathers leave
as if going to work as usual,
can they?
When does a woman know
what to say to her daughters.
Then, too, she was no longer
a corporate lawyer or mother or woman
though she was.
She was falling in love in the mountains
fighting beside her comrade,
Jose Maria Alvarado.
She fought the National Guard
until six months pregnant
when they sent her to Costa Rica
in charge of financing the Southern Front.

I do not know what she was doing
July 19, 1979.
Perhaps in her last trimester
barely able to breathe
she shouted for the grandeur
of the peasants' Triumph.
Perhaps she wept, as I would.
And now with the war
directly against U.S. intervention
she leads Nicaragua's mission to the U.N.
where Nora, a male colleague admitted,
wears her past the way other women
wear perfume;
where, an opponent said,
Norita is a resonance box
and what is put into it
is decided in Managua.
Of course. That's her job.
Though no one would say that
of a man.
As I complete this narrative
I think of all the women
I'd love to fight alongside,
here, North of the Border,
as a gift to Nicaragua.

NOTE: This poem is based on and uses quotes from two sources:
"Nicaragua's U.N. Voice" by Elaine Sciolino (*The New York Times Magazine,*
Sept. 28, 1986). and *Sandino's Daughters: Testimonies of Nicaraguan Women
in Struggle* by Margaret Randall and edited by Lynda Yanz (New Star Books:
Vancouver, Canada, 1981). It is interesting to note that Ms. Astorga was
appointed Nicaragua's chief delegate to the United Nations only after the
U.S. Government rejected her as Nicaragua's ambassador to the United
States in 1984.

Seizure

In Nicaragua
old women
mobilize with sticks and boiling water
again.
You're North American.
You figure it's the season.
But back home
the moon
acts like that girl
who'd been fucked in so many places
she hardly knows which hole
is for babies
and you know you understand

un deber de cantar

and you know you understand
your desire
to see Broadway
NY NY
taken in a flash of July heat
and you know you want it.
(The green parrots snap
guapa
and your thighs sweat like mad.)
And you want it.
Shit. We don't have mountains here.
The rooftops
will do the trick

you think out loud.

Because you belong to a process
that belongs to you

one

you love to touch

and nurse

and deploy

on your lap, here
Nicaragua. On your

lap here Nueva
New York. Here

novio, baby

sister. When I say *mujeres*

man of course

I mean *y hombres*

tambien.
I'll never forget

the shower that riddled the tobacco fields
on the Honduran border of Nicaragua

where Suyapa
una nina de 4 anos

learned June 9, 1983
what somocistas are

—yanquis, contras—
if she didn't know

before she was hit by mortar. Seizure
you envision

as the street
after the water has broken.

Note: *un deber de cantar*, "a duty to sing," is the title poem of
contemporary Nicaraguan poet, Rosario Murillo.

Resistance: a poem on ikat cloth

By the time the forsythia blossomed
in waves along the parkway
the more delicate cherry and apple
had blown away, if you remember
correctly. Those were days
when you'd forget socks and books
after peeing in the privacy
of its branches and soft earth.
What a house you had
fit for turtles or sparrows.
One sparrow
wrapped in a silk kimono
wept for her tongue
clipped off by the old woman.
You'll never forget that
or its vengeance as striking
as the yellow around your small shoulders.

> *shitakirisuzume* mother called her.
> You never need to understand
> exactly.

a technique of resist-dying
in Soemba, Sumatra, Java, Bali,
Timor,

> Soon came mounds of flesh
> and hair here and there.
> Centuries earlier
> you'd have been courted

or sold.

> "Inu has let out my sparrow — the little one
> that I kept in the clothes-basket she said,
> looking very unhappy."

For a eurasian, sold.

> murasaki

mother

> She soaked the cloth
> in incense
> then spread it on the floor
> standing there in bleached cotton,
> red silk and bare feet.

And you fell in love with her
deeply as only a little girl could.
Pulling at your nipples

you dreamt of her body
that would become yours.
      "Since the day we first boarded the ship
      I have been unable to wear
      my dark red robe.
      That must not be done
      out of danger of attracting
      the god of the sea."
red as a Judy Chicago plate
feast your eyes on this
jack
      "when I was bathing along the shore
      scarcely screened by reeds
      I lifted my robe revealing my leg
      and more."
roll up that skirt
and show those calves
cause if that bitch thinks
she can steal your guy
she's crazy
      The cut burned
      so she flapped her wings
      and cried out
      but choked
      on blood.
The thread wound round your hand
so tight your fingers
turn indigo
      murasaki
The Shining Prince realized
he could form her
into the one forbidden him. For that
he would persist
into old age.
      rice starch
envelope, bone, bride
      you can't resist
The box of the sparrow's vengeance
contained evils comparable to agent orange
or the minamata disease. The old man
lived happily
without her. But why her?
except that she was archetypal.
      She depended on her child
      to the point that when her daughter died

and she left Tosa
she could only lie down
on the boat's floor
and sob loudly
while the waves
crashed against her side
almost pleasantly.
This depth lent him
the soft black silt
on the ocean floor
where, all life, some men say, began.
warp
"Mr. Ramsey, stumbling along a passage
one dark morning, stretched his arms out,
but Mrs. Ramsey, having died rather suddenly
the night before, his arms though out,
remained empty."
when the men wove and women dyed
mother —
mutha
Orchids you explained
represent female genitalia
in Chinese verse.
Hence the orchid boat.
Patricia liked that
and would use it in her collection
Sex and Weather.
the supremes soothed like an older sister
rubbing your back
kissing your neck and pulling you into
motor city, usa
whether you liked it
or not that
was the summer
of watts and though you
were in a coma
as far as that
the ramifications
the ramifications
bled through transistors
a *class* act
blues from indigo, reds
from mendoekoe root, yellows, boiling
tegaran wood
and sometimes by mudbath

when you saw her bathing in the dark
you wanted to dip your hand in
mamagoto suruno?
The bride transforms
into an element
such as water
while the groom moves
like the carp
there just under the bridge—
like the boy with you
under the forsythia
scratching and rolling around.
No, actually you just lay there
still and moist.
Wondering what next.

pine.

You're not even certain
which you see—
the carp or the reflection of your hand.
the forsythia curled
like cupped hands covering
bound and unbound
As if blood
"The thought of the white linen
spread out on the deep snow
the cloth and the snow
glowing scarlet was enough
to make him feel that"
The sight of him squeezing melons
sniffing one
then splitting it open in the park
was enough to make you feel that
Naha, Ryukyu Island, Taketome, Shiga,
Karayoshi, Tottori, Izo,
resistance does not mean
not drawn it means
sasou mizu araba
inamu to zo omou
bind the thread
with hemp or banana leaves
before soaking it in the indigo
black as squid as seaweed as his hair
as his hair
as I lick his genitals
first taking one side

deep in my mouth then the other
til he cries softly
please
for days

Though practical
you hate annotations
to the *kokinshu;*
each note pulls apart
a *waka*
like so many petals
off a stem
until your lap
is full of blossoms.
How many you destroyed!
You can't imagine
Komachi's world
as real. Hair
so heavy it adds
another layer of brocade
(black on wisteria,
plum—)
forsythia too violent
and the smell
of fresh *tatami.*
But can you do without
kono yumei no naka ni
Can you pull apart the line
"my heart chars"
kokoro yakeori
corridors of thread
"creating the pattern from memory
conforming to a certain style
typical of each island"
"K. 8. Fragment of ramie kasuri, medium
blue, with repeating double ikat, and mantled
turtles and maple leaves of weft ikat.
Omi Province, Shiga Prefecture,
Honshu.
L. 16.5 cm. W. 19.5 cm."
"the turtle with strands of seaweed
growing from its back forming a mantle,
reputed to live for centuries,"
Komachi also moved
like those shadows in the shallows
you cannot reach

though they touch you.
Wading and feeling
something light as a curtain
around your calves you turn
to see very small scallops
rise to the surface
for a moment of oxygen
then close up and descend.
Caught, you look
at what he calls their eyes
(ridges of blue)
and are afraid to touch
that part.

    from memory or history
sasou mizu

    Grandmother's *ofuro*
    contained giant squid
killer whales
    hot
omou

    You were afraid of him
    turning to the sea
    saying something that would separate you
    forever
    so kept talking.
    Of course he grew irritable
    and didn't really want
    a basket of shells
    for the bathroom.
"his arms though open"
    The line shocked you
    like so much of Kawabata
    who you blame
    for years of humiliation,
    katakana, hiragana, kanji,
at each stroke
    You hear the squall first
    coming across the lake in your direction
    like a sheet of glass.
    You start to cry and daddy
    rows toward the shore and mother.
in the Malayan Archipelago
    George O'Keeffe's orchid shocked you
    so even now you can picture the fragrance
"Should a stranger witness the performance

he is compelled to dip his finger
into the dye and taste it. Those employed
must never mention the names of dead people
or animals. Pregnant or sick women
are not allowed to look on;
should this happen they are punished
as strangers."
                    in the Malayan Archipelago
                    where boys give their sweethearts
                    shuttles they will carve, burn,
                    name,
"language does not differ
from instruments of production,
from machines, let us say,"
                    knocked down
knocked *up girl*
                    "the superstructure"
he wouldn't stop talking
about *deep structure*
                    and mention in prayer
but you need more than the female persona.
A swatch of cloth.
A pressed flower. The taste of powder
brushed against your lips.
                    pine
matsu
                    The wedding day chosen
                    he brought you animal crackers
cloths
                    Pushing aside the branches
                    you crawl in
                    on your hands and knees
                    lie back,
                    and light up.
tabako chodai
                    because the forsythia
                    symbolizes so much
                    of sneakers,
                    cloth ABC books, charms,
sankyu

the "charred heart"
would be reconstructed thus:
"Before the golden, gentle Buddha, I will lay
Poems as my flowers,
Entering in the Way,
Entering in the Way."
                    fuck that shit
Link the sections
with fragrance: *matsu*
                    shards of ice
The bride spread out her dress
for the dry cleaners
then picked kernels of rice
off the quilt and from her hair.
                    bits of china
the lining unfolds
out of the body
through hormonal revolutions
gravity and chance
                    lick that plate clean
can I get a cigarette
                    got a match
click clack, click
clack
                    chodai
in this dream
                    She wrapped the ikat
                    around her waist and set out
                    for Hausa, Yoruba, Ewe of Ghana,
                    Baule, Madagascar, and Northern Edo
I relax, pull off my dress
and run along myself
until dry and out of breath.
                    click clack click
clack
                    and in the rhythmic chore
                    I imagine a daughter in my lap
                    who I will never give away
                    but see off
                    with a bundle of cloths
                    dyed with resistance.

Notes to "Resistance: a poem on ikat cloth"

Ikat: "the technique of resist-dying yarn before it is woven"
(*African Textiles*, John Picton and John Mack, London, 1979).

Line 11	Sparrow references from the Japanese folk tale, "*Shitakirisuzume*" (literally, "the tongue-cut-sparrow"). The sparrow received the punishment after eating the old woman's rice starch. The sparrow got even.
Line 22	Locations in Indonesia known for ikat.
Line 29	*Genjimonogatari (The Tale of Genji* by Murasaki Shikibu, translated by Arthur Waley). This is the first time Genji hears the child Murasaki who he later adopts, then marries.
Line 33	*Murasaki* also means "purple."
Line 45 & 54	*Tosanikki (The Tosa Diary* by Ki no Tsurayuki translated by Earl Miner), written in the female persona.
Line 72	"The Shining Prince" refers to Genji.
Line 100	*To the Lighthouse*, Virginia Woolf.
Line 130	Colors refer to dyes used in Indonesia. (*Ikat Technique*, Charles Ikle, New York, 1934).
Line 135	*Mamagoto suruno*, Japanese, "playing house."
Line 156	*Yukiguni (*Snow Country, *Kawabata Yasunari, translated by Edward Seidensticker).*
Line 165	*Locations in Japan known for ikat.*
Line 169	*Sasou* etc. is a quote from a waka (classical Japanese poem) by Ono no Komachi. Donald Keene translated these lines, "were there water to entice me/ I would follow it, I think." (*Anthology of Japanese Literature* p. 79).
Line 184	*Kokinshu* is the Imperial Anthology of poetry completed in 905.
Line 201	*Tatami*, straw matting for the floor in Japanese homes.
Line 203	*Kono* etc., Japanese, for "in this dream."
Line 205-6	From another Ono no Komachi poem translated by Earl Miner (*Introduction to Japanese Court Poetry*, p. 82).
Line 208	Ikle, p. 50.
Lines 211-19	*Japanese Country Textiles,* Toronto, 1965, p. 16; p. 15.
Line 242	*Ofuro*, Japanese bathtub.
Line 257	*Katakana* etc. are the Japanese syllabaries and the Chinese characters respectively.
Line 279	*Joseph Stalin, Marxism and the Problems of Linguistics.*
Line 293	*Matsu*, Japanese, "pine tree" and "wait."
Line 302	*Tabako chodai*, Japanese, "give me a cigarette [tobacco]."
Line 307	*Sankyu*, Japanese pronunciation of "thank you."
Line 310	Noh play by Kan'ami Kiyotsugu, "Sotaba Komachi" supposedly about Ono no Komachi's repentence. (Keene, p. 270.)
Line 336	Locations in Africa known for ikat.

GALE JACKSON

she.

alone after the lovers leave
the one who comes the one who goes
the one who never stays
she
watches the day break with painful
precision over streets littered
with neglect she longs to ride
the nite foreboding, she longs
to ride the wind.

a poem to begin again.

it begins when the radio shocks you awake
tho the child was beaten to death two years ago
and others still and atlanta and south africa and philly
and time and time shrouds their bodies. another acquittal.
it begins when you get up. shed sleep. dress. go to work.

it begins when you're ready or not. it began long ago
displaced by slavers despised as evidence and strength
roaches run in the damp where pipes are cracked, new york city
sunrise sunset birds in migration and everyday everyday
there are many funerals. it begins as it begins as it never ends.

it begins the day before the last day or the first day of the month
which is mothers day with the women and the women's brown-faced
children and the lines for foodstamps, clinic, housing court
housing the endless lines that begin in early morning that stretch
deep into the dreams. it begins with tears or anger
it begins when you fourteen and pregnant and is on you
and you go on welfare and you stop acting like a child
it begins when you lose your childhood.

it begins on a cold nite no room at the inn just a million
empty windows the star hidden by a counterfeit skyline
it begins when you have no home and the temperature drops
below freezing.

it begins how you work for a living and be living to work
how you stare up at gold mountain and be thrown off when you dare
to climb and not be allowed water on the mountain when you crawl
it begins with thirst and the search for beauty in a sleepwalker's
face, on the bus, looking for it in a face
how you get on the bus tired and you come back home worse
for doing somebody else's work so glad to not be hungry, even
if you thirst, looking for a man or the moon to wink just right.

it begins because you do not have a choice with the woman draping
the danger of nite around her, putting on her heels and stalking
it back. it begins with the stomach unsettled, with a half sharp
pencil with a half dull knife. it begins in your draws. it is not
sexy. it begins with ghosts and then your neighbors and the wailing
of fire engines and the howling of dogs. it begins cause you can't
sleep thru it. it begins with dying, it begins with the will to live.

before five in a shanty or a highrise, with coffee or tea or nothing
all the same because it has never stopped and the world spins and
the old ways burn in the streets or in our hearts. it begins
and even if the radio never came on again you would know to wake up
that another child has passed thru hunger or cold or just plain evil
that you must begin   to stop   that each beginning must matter to make it
that other women men children are waking or sleeping all making it
towards home. it begins where it ends making it towards home.

it begins with a woman looking for a beginning and finding
her own hands a weapon a balm. it begins with or without
chick or child, heat or hot water, contemplating bellevue or
a woman's shelter to escape the cold that's crept in
on the edge, the edges of things where living and dead
walk hand in hand on the far reaches of one imagination
gathering in the skirts of memory crawling or standing
and walking towards someplace no bus goes called home.

coyote is the falling star...a zuni tale.

for david

coyote love to dance is true he dance from day till nite
coyote took to dancin and that dancin be a sight
coyote dance with tortoise and then he might dance slow
coyote dance with prairie dog and then he might step low
coyote dance with rooster and help him get his sound
coyote dance with eagle and his feet don't touch the ground
coyote dance with sparrow and dance way up on his toes
coyote dance with aardvark and get all in her nose
coyote dance with bison and still he beg for more
with little ones like rabbit he dance with three or four
coyote dance with rattlesnake and coil up in her lair
coyote dance with horses and he whisper in they hair
coyote dance with buffalo and never miss a beat
coyote dance with centipede and step on all her feet
coyote dance with sunset till she holler up then down
coyote dance new moon to full and then he go to town
coyote howl for dancin he just cannot get enough
he dance with wolf and bear and deer and no one hang as tough

but when coyote dance with starlite she really take him high
when coyote dance with starlite she spin him cross the sky

when coyote dance with starlite they hustle on the moon
when coyote dance with starlite she sing him a monsoon
when coyote dance with starlite is lightning her fingers snap
when coyote dance with starlite is thunder when she clap
he stood below the sky one nite and stretched up high his paw
he called to north star east and west "i wanna dance some more"
the stars all laughed but they reached down to bring him dance with them
and up he climbed the centuries climbed and danced on heavens brim
starlite dance him thru winter into spring and then cross fall
but tired he slipped thru summer he knew he'd seen it all
he tumbled down seven mountains chasing snowflakes in his fall
he falls thru all the heavens a streak of lite a burning ball
so if you see the sky one nite and if a star falls by
youll know is just coyote been star dancing way up high....

Adapted from N. Belting. *The Earth is on a Fish's Back.*

distances.

for the twins

imagine him a condor
wings a man's height
stairstep on wind
hunted and wild.
imagine him antelope
large as grandfather
oak
the sleeping ones
swiftfoot legs arms
powerful gentle
creature
imagine him
the last one of two
looking back on majestic
mountains torn open
for poison and steel
majestic mountains mute
and the condor
poised before ancestry
wondering what you'll leave
for the centuries to learn
you cry and it
echo on ground water
carry thru valley
what they
have multiplied wrong
and lost
forgetting
the wind is to climb
the land to roam in an embrace
stairstep on wind
your athlete's body
in flight.

the beginning of the story.

for edmund perry.
june 13 1985.

i'm tryin' to find the beginning of the story of the child
i'm tryin' to find the beginning of the story of the child
who became a man in a time of war dividing nothing from plenty
i'm tryin' to find the beginning of the story of the child
who became a man in a time of war dividing nothing from plenty
in a time of hunger as ungiving as concrete in brooklyn
mean as the absence of trees on crosstown streets where there are
no fresh vegetable markets, where there are no stories admitted
only tv where there is living and living in broken glass
and the uncaring smell of piss, beer but no good water, cigarettes
but no crayons, welfare small hopes anger no place to put it
but the belly

i look deep into the story of the child
i look deep into the story of the child who to live had to try
i look deep into the story of the child who to live had to try
harder be tougher be smarter run relays of the imagination against
an undefined line and win, and dream antelope cheetah bird against
roaches and dream grass against piss store like a camel food
for the soul love like plenty color with even the fingers believe
fuck the odds and turn anger into magic into gold.

there is no end to the child's story tho they say it is a hunter's season
and heart like his is worth its weight in gold
there is no end to the child's story tho they say it is a hunter's season
and heart like his is worth its weight in gold his beauty so quick and specific
his laughter crest an octave like no other color from his fingertips turning
anger, magician, black child, into gold, faster, harder, tougher, love his
mother's his father's singular child, mistaken for all their worst fears
mistaken for all their worst lies fears over three hundred years of inhumanity
unadmitted made believe that this child, singular beauty of specifications ancient
that this child was their mugger that this child was their ghetto that this
child was urban blight and crime in the streets that this child was their
scapegoat for all their worst selves unadmitted say that it was this magical
child and they, their police, they, their guns, they, their nite walk scandal
covered up in reams and reams of paper and declarations and treaties broken
and promises hollow as holes they murdered this child. they murdered this child.
in an attempt to kill off his magic.
but this is not the end of the story, i swear to god, this is not the end.

at the crossroads.

beirut
divided unto itself
east from west
and if they come
by sea
grenades explode in
grotesque
shadows
on homemade curtains
and shouts of shrapnel
burst
in the eye of children's
dreams.

the one who sings meets me
in the lamplite city nite
a stump where her arm was
a reflection of a woman's
reflection
a siren of mirrors
her strength
century upon century upon
centuries
beneath her chador
a stump where her arm was
she says she will not
leave
here again.

the one who sings meets me
in the dream of a sleeping city
veiled
her steps muted
in modesty
around us bullet holes line
the walls and militias battle
for surer ground
while mothers run pell mell
thru the street
bearing their possessions
their crying
children.

so much a memory of constant
expulsion
nitely bombing
hushing the children
the one who sings meets me
her palms rough as stone
paved roads
we walk and
pigeons fly from our footsteps
in the dream as over
the flaming roofs of lebanon
stone doves
can find no safe place to
lite
and airborne
echo our chaos.

so much a memory
constant
expulsion
and death's smell
and screaming
and silence
her steps muted
arms olive branch
gesture
and sandy reaches
surround her shore
to her own shore
not metaphor shore
to her own shore
palestine.
and the woman waits
for the modern prophet
to breathe water unto
the flaming roof tops
to quench the thirst and turn
camps of refugees
into new cities promised.

and the woman waits
in the lamplite city
walks in the dreams of sleep
and the faces of earth born
children
blind
or torn

by the schrapnel
in the eye
in the rubble
in the city
whence may come
a prophet
a memory constant
century upon century upon
century
for the city
for a people
a memory constant
in flames.

so there is no poetry in these nites.

for the children of soweto.

i do not speak this language
but another
fluent as hieroglyph
filled with click and bop and guttural sounds
i do not overstand these runnins....

bantu
education
group
areas act
influx
control
displacing
surrounding
intervening
so afrikaners, so apartheid, moves my people.

i do not speak this language
i cry bullets
so young, warriors, they bleed
hippos tore them down
on street corners in school uniform
so these children on the frontline
and even as the fast run and the strong
walk way beyond the shootings these bars
grate against voice like glass grinding
on chalkboard the tear gas and the sirens
and the flashing orange lites threaten
to drive them insane and they bleed
chanting
so to speak in their own language....
ghetto
township
redline
dispossess
gentrify
break
break
break

word…

not this language but another these
runnins the question glances of children
the rumblins of empty stop the word the
appetite for nitewalks or freedom fighters
what you know of the force the power
of the spoken the scratch the beat
they would kill you for ritual knowledge
of the real deal.

so speak to me in my country
in i language in i woman in i
heart so speak to me…word…
the kids cry in new york city
in soweto graffitti me so so speak.

so there is no poetry in these nites
cept the writing on walls. so they tough
but babies. they bleed. policemen hunt them
in brooklyn in cieski in soweto torn down
on street corners and even as the fast run
and the strong walk away gunfire bars grate
against expression policemen hunt them grate
tear gas. chalkboards. school uniforms. sirens
rushing thru my city where liberation is the writing
their words
their writing
tag
on the walls.

housework.

cleaning my floors i search for a clarity in wood
a real see myself in it shine and continuity
(like digging thru to china)
in the news for zimbabwe. i am on my knees before tv
was invented, holy rollin' to the radio, but the newscaster
ignores me. blood soaks the bread blesses the wine bends
the torn heads of roses. north america is the battlefield
in the closing distance of my dreams it marches forward
in concrete. oh where is news from zimbabwe, hidden
in section "b" on page 68? when will i hear
from my people keeping one's home is one's nation
colorful as calypso. i'm sure news awaits me making delicate
arrangements of state.
rebel. rebel. up to my knees in detergent.

my longing for you is a quiet wish between
filthy refrigerator shelves and this case of
a bachelor apartment: a frog waiting to become cinderella
a kiss waiting for me to dig her out of soot and romance
thaws as if it were once a castle of ice inside it
how many lives frozen where dreams slip away
leaving lakes of glass slippers and roaches
run between my poems a fecund existence...
so what if i am just defrosting my fridge?
i do think of love, so what is the proper stance anyway
for a woman alone, i wish the chance to be or not to be
a bitch   in love   a woman   the pain in my head
threatens to rip me apart and expose that you can see yourself
in it shine is deep i say, i sit, i miss you here
undisturbed.

hanging from the window at 180 housewife's habitat
i can see that maria marquesa desotta has been burned out
(there are many forms of death and eviction)
and cars roll by the graveyard unaware that another person
has joined the list of casualties and every harsh word
reaching up toward my fire escape is a tongue of flame
leaving me nowhere to run/ spick/ nowhere to run/ nigga/ no where
to run maria marquesa desotta whose husband and whose child
sit, on the stoop another blockade no where to run and
i'm tryin' to make sense out of all this waiting for the calm breeze
but storm after storm after everyone has taken a drink
i return to my bathroom, take a shit, gain courage.

where is the end of this poem? the economy in a diary
and housework: an obsession a preoccupation like in occupied
territory, like in "someone's livin' in this body" the end
is in the beginning. i'm talking bout basic changes in technology
my mop and my pail out into the streets my love off the ice
(this ain't no vertical thing)
i mean i envision hundreds of rejuvenated domestics marching thru the park
reclaiming the land under our adidas…one's home is one's nation
even invisible behind dark apartments or hung from catwalks like burglars
i got my head out the window and i'm hollering   i know you're there
to meet me downstairs and move on the world city borough prospect park west
an army of busily unemployed as the sun takes it down.

the untitled.

for mrs. king

it's the women
who are left
as we are tonite
you. me.
the women left
holding photographs
missing the gone
the assassinated
burying the dead
quickly
give the heart
of the baby died
to a weak one
so that both
continue
to live.
the mothers
of heroes and martyrs.
the women conscious
of the pain
of losing any child
tho she may look
at the womanchild
and see her husband
not knowing
her own strength.
women
from sophiatown
which is no more
from alexandria
and bedsty still
they remember
like the bronx
never leaves you
the ones
late nite
going off the walls
alone
lonely
very strong
their ghosts remain
even as the cities

are swept away
not fearing blood pus
or maggots
only the absence
of ritual
...kindness
but on these nites
ice cold
crystal clear
they know it
all the way in
bones
deep as sorrow.
it is the women
who are left
in the bantustans
in the ghettos
they do not choose
or name
squatting over some
other people's dead
when the men go
to the cities
to war
insane
when the last good stream
has gone dry
and the check won't
come
when the lovers go
she is left
stop
to sit
be company
for a friend
left
when there is no right.
sleep
for dreams.
and if no one dare
wake her dare break
her pact with god
she may leave and never
return
to this
false version of life
gaining a foothold
she may decide
to soar.

new york. beirut. nagasaki.

Who promises redemption
this is the third day and summer a flare
rising against pavement against tenements
against an african sky
young men in khaki pants look west
to beirut where the many passings fill
the nite with homeless shadows seeking
refuge where walking is a balancing act
and sinners
the ones with real religion.

2.

When pink clouds pass over the habor
over the tankers and conduits eastward
in brooklyn the sky threatens august thunder
storms and the detonation of bombs or anger
bending the clouds into a halo that drifts
liquid over the industrial city
over and over pulling our eyes skyward
walking softly to balance the dance of elements
the ether, the explosive, situation.
i dreamt of crossing a tunnel to her arms
of walking a vast metropolitan horizon
taut as a tightrope before me; the arch
thru a tunnel that is a subway a skyway a silo
the dream, good or ill, extended.

3.

The full moon also rises over beirut
where the dead lay uncounted where the stain
grows and festers like a sore, who can sleep
who dares to tonite as only the stout wind
at the head of a storm can move the garbage over
new york city beirut nagasaki this is the third day
august 9th. a storm is coming tonite tomorrow impending
sure as the universe is its own prediction and
the perpetual sorrow of passed spirits will be heard
once more
and those who know no better will think it inconvenient
but the others, they will know.

a hottentot tale.

for sean

in the beginning
moon...
and sun...
but moon
moon
move up
thru darkness
move up
thru
black
centuries starlite
know the nite...
so moon
moon call up
one
firefly.
moon
tell her say
"bring this word
to the people:
tell them
that as i
moon
dying live
and live
tho i die
so they too
will live still
beyond dying."
moon
tell her say
"take the people
these words."
and so
firefly went
— wings kissing
the sky —
so
firefly went
but before
she got
to the people

was stopped
by hare
who asked:
"where you goin'
one
firefly?"
"i'm bringin'
moon's words
to the people"
she say
"she say
that i should
tell them
that as she dying
lives
and lives
tho she dies
so they too
will
still live
beyond dying"
which hare thought
was good
though he felt that
he should
carry
moon's word on
quickly
cause firefly
be slow
in flying
—wings kissing
the sky—
and she know she slow
so she let hare go
on towards
the village.
and in his haste
it was hare
who brought
this confusion;
who spoke
moon's words
incorrectly.
he say

to the people
gathered up
from near and far
he say
to the people:
"as the moon dies
with the sunrise
so you too
will perish
and be gone"
and believing
this
they went.
and so to this day
the people
people
got it wrong.

---

adapted from P. Radin. *African Folktales.*

home.

for benjamin moloise the poet
and our brothers in the mines

when they leave
those cities
the long nites
underground
the miners return
to lesotho or zimbabwe
or mozambique
or up country
crossing over roads
where there are none
carry the bodies
of slain children
between the mines
and the country
the ports and the landlocked
lips
of home...
in the land of home
no home just a job way
in the land
of screaming ghosts of red rivers
distant ocean false bay in the land
of home...

the day they hung the poet
for crimes against the state
his mother stood outside
prison gates bells tolled
a policeman looked out
said:
"you can go home now
he's dead."
the day they hung the poet
colored children sang
in the white only area
they sang "we are the world"
and botha sent
an army to quell them
nannies
gardeners

domestics
joined them
the unemployed
the prostitutes
the ones just drifting thru
the day they hung the poet
the army came out
for the first time
to quell what had become a riot
on accounta colored children singing
in the heavily guarded area
that the whites call
home.

back towards
mountain valleys
from filthy cities
breath of mines
coal dust diamonds gold
priceless in their lungs
the miners return
across roads
that ain't roads
passing place and place
again, "homelands"
no black man can call
home
dead children tears
sweat slip from the
shoulder
to earth burnt
far and long
the poets
the prophets
the wing span
of a crow
the miners return
deepening the footprints
between the mines
and the country
carrying small
white coffins
death dreams ports
towards the landlocked
lips
of home
of home.

¿dónde está alfredo mendez?

a poet wrote it on
the last standing wall
the demolished building
a testament to all missing
occupants
if no one remembers
it could be forgotten too
soon, what happens, life
passion and perhaps love
in the embrace the miracle
of conception the struggle
to be born alive walking
first communion first love
first vision if no one
remembers what happened here
there alfredo each of us
if no one remembers what
happened what will happen
will be fatal.

winneba.

hold me
hold on
somewhere the nites
throw off winter simply
paint their faces
dance iguana
bellow like frogs
and the women are armed
against the cold.

an old poem. on the road.

for carole.

on the road in the nite
drawn by a long black limousine
we travel towards baltimore
sonorous
like nina sings it
like grass would tell
like rivers whisper
like weeping willow cries
and only time remembers:
white-tailed deer, swallows
skies dark with geese,
buffalo's trail paved over
for this passage
and time to time to the sky
my heart cries "god!" and
stuck in the throat
of no possible answer
it wavers like wind
or exhaust fumes
from the big trucks
in front of howard johnsons
where the signs read
"too far from home"
and this is what has happened
to the food chain
over five million served
but in the ladies room
poised over toilets where
millions of women have not sat
pissing
quickly
swollen like bugs
in fluorescent lite
numb dumb not sitting
over five million are served
standing up
and about to go
go going and then
gone
the way of the wilderness
back to a land called

no permanent place
in cars that spit
their own fire
in front to god outside
i beg for another passage
deepwater, clearsprings
infinite sky slapping me
to my senses
reminding me to think and then
think again
who would have wanted this
wilderness covered in plastic
the ghost fields of barley
wheat and corn stretching back
only into memory
the lamplite slow poison
the times we move thru truly
too terrible for words
and acres and acres before us
road signs simply ticking it off
what a place to be born into
lonesome long stretch
serpent highways snapping
at their own tails.

your poem. once.

on nites too cold for human possibility
i think of the future
and i think of you
undressing. unafraid. this time
illuminated by your eyes like
the soft lite of waning moon
and the heat makes me shiver
as women will.

on nites this cold i think of palestine
of modern diaspora
of thin dark women and children
hushed with an urgency
only those who have lived
by the gun will understand
and on nites this cold i worry
for all the wanderers who just go
when they say home
in a shopping bag or two

i worry on a nite like this
for cabbies for people out here
learning english the city the road
simultaneously
and i keep whispering "be careful"
on nites like this i want
to be following this pretty young
woman and i want to push back
hard
when i'm pushed on nites like this
my tongue is sharp my breath frost
my heart wax melting longing
to take it all into my arms
on nites like this i am the
quintessential lover limited only
by my reach aching to stretch
my arms like wings for flight
to undress fear in the lites and darks
of blackness aching for the nite
streets in new york or capetown
to be mine to be mine i think

like this on nites this cold
i/ wish/ that/ kid/ wouldn't/ steal/that
old black lady's pocketbook/ i/ jus
wish he won't
and is cold unbearable naked as
i am
on the streets where i walk bundled
against the cold when the wind
chill factor mocks our hip hop wisdom
taking cold into deep freeze and ice
into reservations of pain
and we be so separate torn
like dancers on a vast stage

but when all is still on nites like this
i think of freedom the future palestine
south africa how nothing really dies i think
of twilight and the language of the city
and i think of you undressing unafraid
this time illuminated by your eyes
where the vision of the future the freedom
unfolds like the lite of a waning
moon
and the heat gives me warmth
to dream in

days before fall.

for maria victoria

africa...
she from somewhere
else
standing
among the delicacies
she sells
and the softness
in her hair
billows hidden autumn
springs
henna russet gold
ringing at her cheeks
from where it hurts
here
una morenita
una karate instructor
la lucha
springs
a house cat
awakened
from dreams of islands
and continents
and memory echo
at her breasts
she says
that she is sad
—dominica
—guyana
—grenada
and lovers weep
and the season wears
a skirt of trash
a wedding veil
as the wind swirls
high
over this place
these people displaced
and across an ocean
where she has come
and gone
and still remembers

in the accent what
it is
when the waves call you
and the dead whisper
hyacinth into woolly hair
as she sells
the gourmet dishes
spiced
with the colonial
the senegalese
chicken
corn soup hearts
of palm from brazil
as she sells
the gourmet dishes
the tough softness
her hair reminds you
...africa
she from somewhere
else
and that in these days
before fall
the seasons
will change.

guadeloupe.

she came to the pier
weaved her perfume
among the dizzy tourists
and the impatient taxis
and the official vendors'
stalls.
looking for her friend.
"eddie from dominica"
where, the natives boast,
they have sweetest coconut
in the world.
later, the sea between them
before them for now,
they sat in the garden
talking, quick and slowly,
talking, as lovers do.

haiti. new york.

this one morning
the dictator was gone
and brooklyn was singing
this one morning
caught in a flurry
of snow and imagination
down eastern parkway
towards the monument
of an unfinished
civil war.
this one morning
when the dictator
had fled death
with his crossboned
mask
moved over and
the haiti of brooklyn
spilled sweet champagne
into the contradictions
of the tiger's new year
the foam
drowning capsized boats
imprisonment
in their own country
imprisonment here
this one morning
when the dictator was gone
brooklyn wore its creole
manifestos
and the nurses and
the taxi drivers
and all the day maids all
had their day
of blue flags and red
waving
as tho
this one morning
the past could be shooed
with a wave in a
brooklyn snowstorm
and the footprints marching
towards the civil war monument
and the past sent marching
the past sent marching
towards the grave.

love.

faith's landing
is a place
where gunriver falls fall
and your breath is a river
called remembrance
willows weep casting their hair
to northeasterly wind
where you ask
and i answer
yes.

deepwater.

for sara

"i jumped in the river and started to drown
but when i saw you i just couldn't go down"
"deepwater"
can take you out
she said
some people can't help but drown in it.
this is a poem for sara who said "thirst
will bring you to water" got to try to
swim or sink or fly "water to drink."

there are shallow waters
the absence of drought
thin cows gaunt women
long neck fowl.
there are still waters
run deep
muddy bottoms
tears of release or retribution
children you cry for
still bodies so unlike what your water
broke. dry mouths you spit to wet.
there are still waters
damned by resistance.
there are shallow waters
where someone has taken more
more than their share.
there are stagnant waters
where poison waits.
and there are pipelines and faucets
to bring it all home.

my sister in capetown
my great aunt in south orange
has a flush toilet and running water
in the house where she works
for a white woman or she could not stay
in capetown
in south orange
water barely washes
the shit away.

there are endless cycles
embryonic fluids
marriages and wars
there are women walking
fetching water
from a truck a stream a well.
there are women plowing
paths for water.
a stick a hoe a baleful ox.
there are women who search
and women afraid to find
what the red water yields.
a whole continent of women
watching the rivers
for the bodies of their dead.
a whole continent of women
watching the skies, for rain.
to wash
scorched babies bones.
to wet
the mouth of hunger.

you could lose sight of the coastline
and they make you a slave.
this is a poem for a lover.
her lips full of sedition.
she spits when she says apartheid
intervention limited warfare.
she says "swim upstream"
or you bound to die.

she said
that there are bad waters
heavy with armored ships thick
with oil
dock in ports of explosion
false bay
red sea
middle passage
the still angry waters
that bore rum and molasses
and men and women
turned slaves.
there are nuclear clouds
radiation acid rains

undrinkable water
fountains marked "colored"
"white"
where people have died to drink
like landlocked states
battlin for position
sea embargos
that stop the boats with food
mines
in the harbors
soundless waters around
el salvador
water that seen too much
in atlanta
the mississippi
the jordan
heavy with bones
capillaries
flooding the heart...
she said that there are waters
you could drown in
or find the way to swim
how it rushes all around you
how it takes you out
and brings you back
home.

what time abides.

for marilyn

i imagine you barefoot
toes dangling over an incline
breeze playful in your hair
"this is no laughing matter"
you laugh a lizard's tongue
darting colored threads into
this fable this form this
fallacy turned inside outside
rightside staring it down
the precipice. what the seasons know
we learn slowly. time has shown us
too much to refuse us but too little
to abide.

SUSAN SHERMAN

Definitions

1.
I think it's coming close to death
that does it
        both others
      & your own
that magnifies the values
begins the definitions

This morning
        mild at last
     after weeks of chill
Streets heavy with water
People stepping
        cautiously
    hardly knowing where
    to place their feet
so accustomed to barriers
           of salt and ice

My mind resembles those winter streets
grey
    with sludge
The snow cover melted
The sidewalks washed of unfamiliar
glare

2.
After all   she said
What difference does it make?
That's the reason I never write
hardly speak   of what is me

I begin to answer glibly   stop
Held myself in identical fear
My own touch tentative
          almost an excuse
like making love to someone
for the first time
or the third (which is always harder)
once you begin to know   experience
another

the tension of your hair   brown
streaked with grey
                    the lines of
your face   like wires   rushing through
my hands   the pressures of your past
your forehead   your knees

3.
Warm outside   the steam
continues   forced by habit
I open the window   throw the
oracle   trace the heat
The heart thinks constantly it says
One constant then   the heart   another
the drawing back
                    Four o'clock
two hours till dawn   Nightmare
image   your face
surrounded by strangers
Beloved   you turn
                         away
Sweat mixes with flowered sheets
The constant fear
                    To push out
                    finally   cautiously   tentatively
                    and find

                         an empty place

4.
Death brings us close to it
Death itself
                    forgetting
And we the living
wanting to remember
not wishing to be forgotten
                              separated
from what we hold most near

I hold you for a moment   lose you
watch you disappear
                         I hold you
for a lifetime   lose you

the next year   the next morning
the next minute   the next breath

5.
You tell me
What can I say to that
young woman 18 years
of age?

That I at 38 must once more lay aside
all sense of definition   order
Must once more carefully measure
the accumulation of my years

Or should I say
her question can be answered
in specific needs   others
and her own
                    But she's asking
more than that   We both know
what she means

The only real difference being death
The one who stops the heart

Ten Years After

1.

How does one find words to speak the things that are
too large for words. How does one fit an idea into
a page, a feeling into a syllable. A room is not a
world. A city is not a continent. These streets
do not border the edges of a universe. But the
people who move in them, the people who live in
them are a world, a continent, a universe.

There were things I never learned, even though I
began, a little, to reach out, to believe I could
reach out.

Ten years. What does it mean? Ten years. *Elegua*.
Guardian of the paths. Opener of the Doors. Trickster.
The Juggler. The Balance. The Fool. The way the world
goes past our understanding, resolves itself in our
blood. How we play out our days, something very great,
and something very small.

The image of the sea comes too often. The city is
another voice. My own body a boundary harder to
resolve. Life is a series of choices. By which we
include or exclude all we ever hoped for or dreamed
of. Love is a series of choices, by which we
include or exclude the world.

2.

If I could speak in the images of dream. If I could
play the words, stretch them across a mile of thought.
Say it has been so long since I have allowed myself
to feel that now I feel too much.

But the words of a poem are silent, make no sound.
Reach across space hands cannot touch. Part of me
has grown old seeing how people move. At different
intervals. At different speeds.

Sometimes, at night, when I am alone, I hear a voice
that calls my name. I am haunted by the memory of
every person I have ever known, will ever know. I am
haunted by the presence of every person I have ever
loved, will ever love.

If I could mold myself into a poem, shape myself into
a syllable, a group of words. What would it mean?

My memories are ghosts which surround me as I write.
My future lies before me like a kind of space. I
would ask for a different sense of timing from the
world, knowing full well, at that moment, time
itself would end and motion cease.

3.
What does it mean to lose. To invest in loss. To
invest in the possibility of loss.

We move from a sense of need. Both others and our
own. But what we move toward is what moves us most.

The wasted days, the wasted hours, the piles of
waste that make up much of our lives, that are part
of our lives. The time lost. The time spent. The
time destroyed.

I want to wake up. Rise up. I want to be awake.
To see.

I had almost forgotten what it was like to be next to
someone, to be warmed by them. To feel warm. I think
of death, more than anything else, as a very cold
place. As a place where contact ceases, where a world
ends.

I know what it is to lose contact. To see the world
grow smaller and smaller. To be unable to reach out.
To be unable to speak. I know what death is like,
what it means.

As everything begins to fall away.

4.
I would like to write a poem that could solve the world,
could solve my place in it. Could make my fantasies
into something real. But I know a poem, words, even
these words, as they come, from my pen, as they sing,
as the poem always sings, as words are used, as motion,
as change.

I know a poem can do none of these things.

Cannot stop the minutes, cannot turn even one hour,
cannot bring into being what does not exist.

Because in all these years, with all this strength
that has grown up in me. With all these words that
have grown up in me. I still cannot find speech
to say what it is I feel, when I really care.

5.
If a poem were a hand, if it were alive, warm. If it
could reach out. If it could enter places I cannot.
If it could do things that make me afraid.

There is this thing that changes, that allows change
to exist. The poem is part of it, is its voice, this
thing that is.

Any struggle is first that deep feeling that grows
from the center of a person, a people. The poem is
not separate from me, from the person I am. It is
not the poem, but I who feels. It is not the poem,
but I, who loves.

To hope, to have hope, to be hopeful, to hope against
hope, to believe in change, to believe in the possibility
of change, to know when to stay. And when to leave.

6.
To discover people is to discover a world. To find
out what is important and what is not.

What does it mean to open yourself, to become open,
to feel. What does it mean to open yourself to other
people, to allow them to enter, to allow them to become
part of your life.

The mountain stands still; above it fire flames up and
does not tarry. Strange lands and separation are the
wanderer's lot.

I am driven by love, *Elegua*. I am driven by love. I
cover my madness, *Elegua*. I cover my pain. Make a
place for me in your house. Protect me as I move.
Elegua. *Elegua*. Guardian of the Doors. Opener of
the Paths.

Cover my years. *Elegua*. Cover my years.

What I Want

I want to be free of all the things that
encumber me   of rent & bills   of tomorrow's
breakfast   of yesterday's words
of my fantasies of love   my insatiable
need for love
I want to be free of the knowledge
of things   of my own shape   my structure
of "that's just not the way it's done"
or "if only you'd done it differently"
I want to be free of time   its endless
repetitions   of myself   my name
names   labels   what defines me
I want to be free of others   of their
distinctions   of my need for them
of this poem   words
I want to be free of newspaper headlines
the radio   television   all these things
that encumber me
Please for a moment relieve me of
constant discovery   this prison
perception   But I am grounded in myself
this world I was born to   my passion
for change   to change things
the need to touch   hold   be touched
held

The Desert & The Sea

What I heard on the roof finally
(being frightened
thinking of burglars   rapists
being murdered in my sleep)
was merely seagulls nesting
The dull roar outside
                                    not cars
but ocean
Not sharp and sudden
A constant sound

A constant sound
the sea
Fading
        then growing louder
wave by wave
Gulls rest on its surface
Two young women walk along its shore
A sensual thing
                        not human
A texture
(Or different textures really)

In the desert
The earth seems still
moving too slowly for human eyes
or lives to follow
The mountains like a barrier
hold everything in place
solid   impenetrable
absorbing
            reflecting
sound
Everything moves around them
The clouds in succession   the rain
then sudden light
                        and then again
the clouds
Birds sing
            and in the night
and sometimes even in the day
crickets squeak their own loud song

I have always fancied myself
an ocean person
Born in July
Cancer the crab
addicted to water
                    and the movement
of things
No earth in my chart at all
Fire water air

I find these mountains have a strange
appeal to me
like something I have been missing
a part
        I have been denied

I don't know how long crabs live
out of water
Even the real things sometimes
burrow themselves
                    deep
in sand
Perhaps to dream of other regions
other worlds
            or just absorb the heat
enclosing themselves in yet another
type of shell

Wherever I have lived
I have always faced the sea
confronted it
            everywhere
Comforted by it   threatened by it
Its symbols surround me
                        fill my dreams
Water wears all else down

But here in New Mexico
Mountains before me
The ocean far away
A new reality claims me

                    earth
                    silence
                    the shifting
                    of light and breeze

Washington D.C./A Study in Black & White

1
Monumental   this seat of government
seat of power
"The throne whereon the monarch sits"
empty
        or seemingly so
not person
            building
this chill Spring
glistening in early afternoon sun
where human act becomes
object
        a frozen thing

To see it is to understand
(nothing walks here
                    nothing moves)
To comprehend with vision
Take it in with the eyes
Examine this city as a work of art
a philosophical concept
a graveyard of classical suspense
centuries out of date

Washington D.C.
Tomb of unyielding laws
monument to abstraction
to rigid perspective
                muted tone
to dead heroes & ancient tales
(always of warriors   always of men
perfectly proportioned   perfectly still)
monument to the universal
what is out of time
to the ascendency   the omnipotence
not of order
            of law

2
March 27, 1982
we protest yet another unjust war
walking the periphery of the ghetto
to Dupont Circle
                    (appropriate name)
the dividing line between
Black and white

We should have stayed there today
in Malcolm X Park
Instead of a "symbolic beginning"
it should have been the end of it

Someday we'll learn
                        always expecting
always wanting to be heard by
the halls of justice
the walls of state
the ones who run things
the "important folk"

Our final destination
Lafayette Park
                    across the street
from the grandest building
of them all
The White House
                        & it is white!
The whitest place I've ever seen
A white that stops you
freezes you in place
Amazing white   spotless white
So white you can barely see its seams

3
If history teaches us anything
It teaches us
                    about direction
space
The poor in Central America
circling the cities
like a giant necklace
                        a choker
How the lines of a drawing
define its shape

4
Washington D.C.
a study in Black and white
neo-classical in style
designed to dwarf you
make you feel small

A model for our future
A masoleum surrounded
                    by living
active need

In its center
the Washington monument
perfect symbol   sharp-edged spear
A missile tens of dozens of years
before its time
Not sex
          weapon
The ultimate offense

Later   on the bus ride home
newspapers swirl through deserted
New York streets
But there is more energy here
in this refuse
more action in the wads
the waste
              & less to fear

than in that tomb to eternity
that shrine
that rules our lives
that sets our days
that governs us
                    or tries

Scene

There is too much misery
in this city
        too much
pain
A dream last night of trains
Trapped in the entrance
pinned
My path blocked
by strangers
Too many of us forced
to breach
the same space

& yet   as I walk along
the street
I am startled by a tree
its bare twigs
        full of
bright red berries
As if someone had placed
them there
to decorate
        the morning

Spring Song

Let's put it another way
The street breaks with ice
It is cold tonight   quiet
This first day of spring

Burdened with clothes
I would shed them   My coat
long blue wraps me into
                              myself
Holds me together

How much we are lied to
Lie to ourselves
How much we hide   How many things
are hidden
                    in these layers
of cotten wool rayon
skin

I am startled by differences
a lack of correspondence
As I was before by what
                              binds us
But things change
Ten years   twenty   thirty
Some drop away   others grow
stronger
                Faces change
& names
I change   remain
What makes us unique

This first day of spring
alone   I wrote
                    this poem
patched a coat of words
stitched a song
Tried to find out what is beneath it
what it means
At the end of it
                    finally
what I would want
to say

This woman tried to grasp life
balance her days
                    the worlds
that sprang
from her hands
broke   from her lips

She was burdened as we all are
by ends and beginnings
But she never turned away

Morning Poem

There's always plenty of time
until it runs out on us
But you can't rush things either
They grow at their own speed
reaching for a point of contact
of their own

I am plagued with impatience
inertia
          the two extremes
the edges of everything
Those two things also
being one

Some people build homes   houses
of themselves   I think of Jung
his circular walls
                    years of
thought enclosing his body
Trapped in his own ideas

Others travel the streets
planting themselves in their
sidewalks
            Their bodies a motion
more like a dance

And some try both worlds
multiple existences
                    are makers of life
Patience is part of it   but more
To have a vision   To make it
real

      Can you see what I'm saying
How time itself is our enemy
our friend   How we trap ourselves
in vision
            But how it also opens
                              out
can lead us forward

How we lose things only to find
them again
                Only to find ourselves
different   at the same place

Listen   this morning the world closes
and opens at my fingertips   The sun
is bright   draws me to it
But I sit in a room cluttered with
memories books old pieces of furniture
old pieces of myself

I am inside
                and outside
of it all
I reach out
with what is behind me
I live my death
                    am captured
in my life

Facts

1
What you see is what you get
What you hear is
                    often lies

Burnt out buildings
on Ave C
Speculators buy and sell empty shells
where people used to live
& still do
            illegally now
among the ruins

I used to live there once
on Ave. C
twice really — at different times
1963   1971
chased out finally by rats
& thieves
                    & a man's throat cut
in front of our building
on an otherwise pleasant summer night

Most important
I was lucky —
I had somewhere else to go

The neighborhood hasn't "gone up"
since then
regardless of what the papers say
It's gone down
Down to money
                    & greed
disregard for human needs
& illusion

That "things are getting better"
At least for some

4
"Why?" is not "How?"
is not a recital of physical causes
physical effects
It is meaning

The bullet pierced her flesh
because a finger pressed a trigger
& she was in the way
is "how"
Why that gun was there at all
why she was in front of it
why that policeman's finger pressed the trigger

not muscles   but years are behind the answer
not reflexes
                people

5
I clip the photo from the paper
pin it on my wall
rip the caption into shreds

Apartheid
                what it means

Separation

Separation from land
Separation from family
loved ones
                education
                home

                Apartheid
                                facts left undefined
that lead nowhere
that separate us
rob us
        of meaning

Apartheid
It destroys us all

2
South Africa
                September, 1984
A story in the *New York Times*
South Africa
                40 miles south of Johannesburg
28 dead
600 detained in one weekend
Picked up at the funerals of their loved ones
and their friends
The photo shows death
                        rebellion
Black people moved again
as they were before
and before
and continue to be
(except in our press)
                to action

Resisting
the lie

Underneath the photo — a caption
No explanation   A statement of fact
A lie of omission
"Police Quell a Riot"
as if implying they were doing
a commendable
                act

So many injured
So many killed
& how many times in our papers
do they tell us

"Why?"

3
In my class I ask
"What is a fact?"
A student answers
"What you hear on the 5 o'clock news."

I laugh   but it isn't funny
& I am the only one
who gets the joke

6
October 6—
"Pretoria Will Use Army to End Riots"
"Military called in to support the police"
80 now are dead

October 23 —
2 o'clock in the morning   7,000 South African soldiers
(along with police) surround a town
Standing 20 feet apart
guns in hands
Two more townships follow
over 150,000 Blacks are interrogated
Their hands are stamped
Their thumbs dipped in orange ink

A general strike is called   succeeds
Now whites also are detained
In Soweto
The people continue to rebel
In Soweto
The people continue to fight back
In Manhattan
My student looks at the 5 o'clock news

His head is filled with facts
He knows nothing
He learns nothing

He doesn't even know *"Why?"*

From Nicaragua A Gift

for Margaret Randall

If you were to ask me
to name a color for that land
I would say it was green
But the color you sent was yellow
A plane descending into green
The sun rising golden beyond its wings

Many things are made of gold
A voice sometimes is known as golden
A wedding ring
                    Even silence
(when chosen)

But "to be silenced"
That's a different matter
That's to choke on one's own words
erupt in violence
                    an act of war

Margaret   today   in your letter
folded in a press release
COVERT ACTIONS AGAINST NICARAGUA
CHALLENGED BY INTERNATIONAL LAW
a small shard of foil falls out
slips to the floor
                    I can't make it out
It puzzles me
What is it?   What does it say?
A rectangular shape   in the center
a golden face
circled by yellow   edged by red
—a cigar band —
                    a cigar band?
Sol Habana
The Havana Sun

Margaret   in the midst of war
both yours & ours
How my country is trying to silence yours
How the silences here are many
& growing
            & the violence
not limited by nationality borders names

How people are more and more refusing
to be silenced
                    in both our lands

Margaret   in the midst of war
from your letters of anger
                            & triumph
death struggle hope
you have sent me/shared with me
perhaps even as an afterthought
who knows?
                (& I will treasure it always)
a gift of light

A Fare/well Present

Well   good-bye
and all that means
if in fact it means
anything
         words sometimes
taking the place
of meaning
            like last night
twisted in my own
syllables   trying
to explain

Or that summer
seven years old
first time away from home
A feeling of the heart
but literally that
            The camp director
calling it "homesick"
or "missing"
Not only that something
was missing
           that I was missing
someplace or someone
but that somehow
I was also missing
from something   somewhere
I wanted to be

A seven-year-old pride
denied it   denies it still
but now with how much more vehemence
command of language
skill with words
            no longer only
(shoulders out   chest squared)
"homesick   not *me*"
but paragraphs of explanation
reams of words
           to say only
somewhere something
has been left out
is out of place

And so   as a farewell present
I give you this poem
This feeling of the heart
That when I think of you
leaving
            And when I think of you here
and can't be with you
Even when we are together
when I feel you growing distant
I experience that
                    "missing"
that something
left out
as if I am discovering the word again
for the first time
What it really means

As with all things that move us
deeply
            the feeling comes
                                    first
the experience
As we perceive the meaning
The word
            follows later
"missing"

that space which is not empty
but fills all space

The Meeting

1.
To touch your face
To touch your arms
To touch your waist
To touch your thighs

To touch your sex

To hold it soft against my cheek
To breathe it slow against my lips
To hold you close against my breast

My love

2.
Old as the woman moaning songs
from her chill staccato walls
Old as that   The touch between us
The chant filtering through coarse
night sounds   The touch between us

Can I name you   The words that lie against
me   Soft against the night   Can I call you
The night itself close upon my thighs

To hold you near
To touch your lips
To hold you close as my own breath

3.
Touched so deeply that tears come
unnoticed   And without pain   That once
were central   And only pain

It is here between us   Not ourselves
But what is here   In this space

Touched so deeply that love comes
unnoticed   And without pain   That once
was central   And only pain

4.
Rain glides in two dimensions   The window
holding it to my face   As I hold you   As I
place my knuckles to your forehead   Moving from
my touch

The vision   two dimensions   The surface
rigid   As we reach toward it   To find it
different   But still there   cool   under
our touch

5.
I would hold you gently
Throw myself against you as
the rain   Talk to you of
small things   As you would
touch a child   Or yourself
small and vulnerable to even
the slightest breath

6.
No longer afraid   The touch of you deeper
than any fear   Deeper than your naked form
The single syllable of your name

As I touch your body
As I touch the earth
As I touch this paper
As I touch each word

It is everywhere   This night and the
outline of our form   As we are together
Without boundary   Without dimension

As I touch the depth of you
My love

Opening Stanzas

for Colleen

It is harder to write of what
is complete
than what is empty
                    We tend
to fill in spaces
avoid confrontation with meaning
outside ourselves

It is the smell of my room
of what has passed between us
that moves me
Not these words
                    or the dozens
I have discarded

How can I say what is contained for me
in the fold of your lip
The way your body leans
                            when you dance
What one remembers finally
are the small things
The tangible remains:
a list (unfinished)   a bottle
of perfume   two magazines
a pair of boots
a row of vitamins on the
kitchen shelf
                    The daisies
I bought you   balanced
lightly   against blue glass

My past rests on the surfaces
of my mind   For me now
the only reality
is our present/presence
together

You fled the seasons
wound up in L.A.
a city I had deserted
years before
                    In New York
I welcomed snow as miracle
The way one accustomed to endless day
(where things pass constantly
but never change)
                              welcomes
the miracle of night

There are no words adequate for it
For what is between us
They will come later
These are   after all   only
opening stanzas
                         welcome as miracle
As I welcome you
pressing into me
draining my emptiness
As together we re-awaken meaning
in small things

                    For you
perhaps   in the seasons
As through you
                         I burst forth
once more
into the sun

The Fourth Wall

1

From which direction does the wind flow? It flows from the East.
From which direction does the wind flow? It flows
from the East and into my hands.

Analysis. Cross-reference analysis. The age of analysis.
Psychological, philosophical, poetic analysis. Not the
event, but the picturing of the event.

Days, dwarf-like, with tinsel hats. America. Orange.
sticky, matted.

My father was from Russia. When he was a small child, he
crossed the borders of his country with a half-dozen other
refugees. He often spoke of the town in which he was born.
A small town. Long rows of hot, sandy streets. Plain
one-story buildings. The cries of Cossacks cutting through
the level dirtwalks of his home.

"Jew," they yelled, and he ran. "Jew," they yelled, and he
ran across a continent. "Jew," they yelled, and he ran
across an ocean.

They never really believed they had left for good. They
never even learned to speak the language. But my father
learned. When he was twelve, he learned — my mother waiting
for him across the length of a continent.

How many years does it take? In this, my sweet-smelling land.
In this, my sweet-smelling land, where there is no
question of time.

They say a desert is an uncultivated region without inhabitants;
a wilderness. A dry barren region largely treeless and sandy.
This is only partly true. My desert is decorated with
pinecones and exotic spice. In spring, the cactus blooms into
small, pink flowers. My evenings are colder than it is
possible to imagine. I take off my clothes at night so I may
lie naked. Next to the warm body of my desert. My beautiful,
beautiful desert.

2

This morning I had a dream. But I have already forgotten. "Yama." "Yama." Hanging to her grandmother's brightly colored skirts. "Watch out for the cars." The rolling cars, with their brightly colored skirts.

That wasn't the way it was, but it was the way it might have been. The roads, long, curved. The roads that curled into the desert. The roads that curled around that patch of land, tying it like a Christmas package with light and warmth and

This morning I had a dream. The bus traveled to the edge of a large, blue lake. Not across roads, but through fields and tall, thin arms of grass.

"Yama," she called, and the call curled around me. "Yama," she called.

Los Angeles is situated in a basin. A flat, grey basin surrounded on four sides by mountains. One of the sides folds down long banks into the sea. Every year or so a part of this fourth wall collapses.

From which direction does the wind flow? It flows from the sea. From which direction does the wind flow? It flows from the sea and into my hands.

San Francisco is water and, crossing the bridge, patterns of lights. Lights suspended on air, on water. And on clear days, rows of hills with houses clutched to their sides. There is a vastness about the land, about the coast. Everything seems too large, unmanageable, like objects to the hands of a small child. The East Coast is different, and New York is cluttered and the distance across the palm of the hand.

Los Angeles, San Francisco, New York. The fourth wall is of an indeterminate size and shape. A desert. An impartial country where the other three are joined together. Every year or so part of this fourth wall collapses.

3

Clear, the music cries and circles the empty space. Clear and compact like a tightly resolved dance. Like this first afternoon as I wander the streets, as others do, as I see it in their faces also, as I walk. New York. Different as it is now, on this first day of warmth.

Clarity is much to be desired and simplicity is the essence
of God. These the words of the Saint. Clarity is much to be
desired. Clarity is much... to be...

Whose feet are these that walk along the streets? Whose
hands hang down from whose body? These are my feet, my hands,
my body. This is my face. The face of the blocks as they
pass. In face of the blocks as they pass. In face of these
members of my body, my face faces the street. The blocks
are passed.

4

They said it was the best our country had to offer. Of itself,
with no intrusion. Behold, here is the land. Behold, here
is the school. Behold, here is the fist, bulging, its muscles
veined with the gold of the earth.

But it was not the earth of which they spoke. It was
the blood of the earth, cut from its body. Los Angeles.
Gigantic. Now red. Now purple. Now the Virgin Mary on the
boulevard, white and yellow lightbulbs falling from her
lips.

I said I did not understand. They said I was young, it was
a matter of growth. Of growth. Of learning how to wield the
sickle, spread the refuse out, side by side, with the long,
uneven rows of grass. When the settlers first came it was
a barren country—a desert surrounded by deserts. They
brought the stucco and concrete. They brought the horses and
the children. They rode over vast ranches of cattle and grain.

This, my father, is what I am. Because one day I stumbled
and scarred my knee so that now, twenty years later, I can still
see the small white dots standing out against my leg. And
after that how hard I found it to walk on your streets.

*I took a brush. It was red. I took a brush. It was green,
orange, yellow. I took a brush. It was the width of the
desert. And into this city I was born and first heard my
name.*

When you are grown your brush will be red—the color of this
city. You will live here, work here, be married here, raise
your children here. You will die here.

I will not die in this city. I will not be the color of this
desert, cut down the middle with blood.

It was raining when I left and raining when I arrived. The streets, the houses, the color of rain. When I was a child I wanted only two things—I wanted to learn and I wanted to write.

This is the way the lesson goes: in that first city there were shapes, huge and grotesque. In the second there was water, and the land like an arm extended to the sea. The third was built on a rock that could not support its own weight. There were people. The people that built the city. And there was the fourth...

Long rows of tightly corseted women through the wide, flat streets. Nothing in that hot sun that was not bright, not stripped with color. And the eyes. Always the eyes. Dressing, living, speaking, fucking for the eyes.

My father, my mother, my country. The dream that my country provoked in them, in me. This is what you made me. What I am. You gave me eyes and hair. You gave me a body. You sent me out—not as one person, but as a group of people, living under the same skin, gathered together under this union of eyes, hair, body. You gave me a name and you robbed me of that name. You gave me all these things and robbed me of them. But you could not take from me what was never yours to give.

I will not die in your city. I will not be buried under
your streets. I will not dress myself in your houses of
gold and lies and grotesque forms.

Always you will live here, close as the blood that flows through the veins of my hand. As I walk into the desert. Father, mother, country. The dream clutched tight to my body, like a lover.

Rituals/A Turning Back

I don't like it (never did)
looking back
                    revising old rituals
renaming old gods

For years now I've been trying to void
my own past
Not because it was bad
Precisely
                    the opposite
Telegraph Ave   a rooming house
no longer there
A 5 o'clock tortilla
washed down with random mugs
of beer — less than a dollar then
(I mark the years as we all do now
by the rise in what it costs
to live)

I can still see that old apartment
It invades my dreams
                        Ornate drawings
decorating walls ceiling floor
A dragon with a tortured smile
A field of grass covered with small
blue weeds
                    (red sky/purple trees)
A house slanted 40 degrees to nowhere
supported by vermillion bricks
                                    & space
Home of cracked gray paint & unlocked door
of first love & sometimes
of violence
                    & often of pain

I don't like it   turning back
never did
                    Nostalgia leaves me cold
The truth is even then I didn't want
to stay
            Wanted to move on

It's twenty-five years now
and part of it I have neatly packed away
part of it surpressed
But there is this other part
that tugs at me
                         ceaselessly
like an angry child
abandoned

demanding attention
demanding to be recognized
demanding to be heard

A Small Question

Don't look for me in the sky
my head is not made up of smoke or
light   but ordinary things
My heart is not tidy
not clean around the edges
Don't look for me under the sea
I walk on land as we all do
make the same mistakes
Don't look at me as distance
I am here   beside you
Please don't change the order
of words   Caring is not possession
All need is not demand
It is not only what we take in
that heals us   but also
what we eliminate
Please pardon me   if I continue
to believe in love

Alchemy

You can't just replace things every time
the pressure mounts
                      memories go wrong
Discarding people
like used-up lives

Sickness plays that role in life
robbing us of desire
setting us adrift
blinding our past
As we also will our own deaths
year after year
                     manufacturing pain
mistaking motion for progress
In order to forget

Dearest friend   Don't leave me now
Just as we begin
Remember the first rule of alchemy
"It can't be done alone"
A lifetime is rarely enough
much less the moment we have left
to find   together
for both of us
through you
                myself
where we each dwell

needing more than anything
time

Lilith of the Wildwood,
of the Fair Places

And Lilith left Adam and went to seek her own place
And the gates were closed behind her and her name
was stricken from the Book of Life

1.
And how does one begin again

(Each time, each poem, each line, word, syllable
Each motion of the arms, the legs
a new beginning)

women   women surround me
images of women   their faces
I   who for years   pretended them away
pretended away their names   their faces
myself   what I am   pretended it away

as a name exists to confine to define confine
define   woman   the name   the word   the definition
the meaning beyond the word   the prism   prison
beyond the word

to pretend it away

2.
Its the things we feel most
we never say   for fear perhaps
that by saying them the things we care most
for   will vanish
Love is most like that   is the
unsaid thing behind the things we do
when we care most

3.
to be an outcast an outlaw
to stand apart from the law   the words
of the law

                outlaw
                    outcast

cast out   cast out by her own will
refusing anything but her own place
a place apart from any other
                        her own

I do not have to read her legend in the ancient books
I do not have to read their lies
She is here   inside me
I reach to touch her

my body my breath my life

4.
To fear you   is to fear myself
To hate you   is to hate myself
To desire you   is to desire myself
To love you   is to love myself

Lilith of the Wildwood
Lilith of the Fair Places

who eats her own children
who is cursed of God

Mother of us all

Love Poem

if I could hold you
if I could wake up in the morning
and see your face
if I could touch you
if I could see you as you go to sleep
if I could feel you close
beside me   if I could reach out to you
touch you   in my need

time drifts endlessly   like water
like this afternoon
the breeze as it drifts
through my window
surrounds me   as thoughts of you
as breath of you
as I see you
as I wait for you
the inevitability of you
as I am surrounded by you
by my love of you
as I waken into life

my words   in silence
my love   in silence
the quiet of the afternoon
the curve of your face
your features   the way
you talk   the way you drift
in my thoughts   endlessly
like time

if you were to ask me what defines me
how I place myself in the world
I would say this poem
is the center of it   is the core
that I reach toward the world
as I reach toward you
as one who wants to reach out
endlessly   who wants to open out
endlessly   who wants to feel
endlessly   that question
that is our lives

KIMIKO HAHN   Photo: Colleen McKay

GALE JACKSON   Photo: Colleen McKay

KIMIKO HAHN was born July 5, 1955, in Mt. Kisco, New York, eventually making her way to New York City via Iowa City. In New York, she studied Japanese literature at Columbia University and received a Masters Degree. She cut her political teeth at the American Writer's Congress and *Artists Call Against U.S. Intervention in Central America*. She was a poetry editor at *Bridge: Asian American Perspectives* and edited the Asian Women United's poetry anthology. Her poems have appeared in *The Agni Review, Bomb, Lips, IKON, Conditions, Blind Alleys, Columbia, The South Dakota Review* among others. At present she coordinates the multicultural reading and workshop series. *Word of Mouth*, in the Chinatown Public Library and is working on a performance piece about a homeless poet. A collection of her poetry is forthcoming from Hanging Loose Press. In spite of — or perhaps, because of — a two-year-old daughter and another child on the way, Kimiko struggles to keep politically active along with her husband, Ted.

GALE JACKSON works in the book arts. She is a poet, a writer, a storyteller, a librarian and an organizer in cultural education. Her work has been published in *Callaloo, Minnesota Review, Freedomways, IKON, 13th Moon, The Black American Literature Forum, Essence Magazine, Obsidian, Azalea, Salsa Soul Gayzette, Sunbury, Conditions* and *The Women's Quarterly Review*. She has co-edited a collection combining literary and visual art from north america with testimonies from Southern Africa: *Art Against Apartheid: Works for Freedom*. She also regularly reviews children's books for *School Library Journal*. She is a co-coordinator for *Art Against Apartheid*: a coalition of artists and arts organizations doing educational work on Southern Africa, and has lectured on progressive cultural work as well as on educational resources, particularly for African american children. Currently, she is working as a reference librarian and instructor at Medgar Evers College of the City University of New York in Brooklyn, New York and near home. Among other current works are a bibliography on African american women writers for a soon-to-be-published collection of essays and the progress of her own novel: *the precision of the embrace*.

SUSAN SHERMAN   **Photo: Colleen McKay**

JOSELY CARVALHO   **Photo: Colleen McKay**

SUSAN SHERMAN is a poet, essayist, and editor of IKON magazine. Beginning in the Sixties she was active in the poetry scene in New York — writing, reading and organizing poetry series at the *Deux Megots* and *Le Metro* — was poetry editor and wrote theatre and book reviews for the *Village Voice* and had nine plays produced off-off Broadway. She taught at the Free School and the Alternative University and took part in *Angry Arts Against the War*. During that time she edited the first series of *IKON*. She was awarded a CAPS poetry grant (1976/77) and editor's awards from CCLM (the Coordinating Committee of Literary Magazines) in 1985 and NYSCA (the New York State Council on the Arts) in 1986. She has published three collections of poetry and a translation of a Cuban play, *Shango de Ima* (Doubleday) and has been published in *Poetry, El Corno Emplumado, Heresies, Conditions, Sinister Wisdom, The Nation, The American Poetry Review* among other journals as well as many anthologies. She is completing a manuscript the "Color of the Heart," a collection of essays and poems and is working on an "autobiography of events." Currently she teaches at Parsons School of Design.

JOSELY CARVALHO, born in Brazil, has been awarded several grants: the New York Foundation for the Arts, 1986-1987; New York State Council for the Arts, Artist-in-Residence, 1978-82; and the National Endowment for the Arts, Community Artist-in-Residence, 1975-76. The founder of the Silkscreen Project at St. Marks's Church in the Bowery, she has had individual exhibits in Latin America and the U.S., including Casa de las Americas, Havana, Cuba, 1986; Yvonne Seguy Gallery, New York, 1983; Central Hall Gallery, New York, 1982 & 1985; Paco das Artes, Sao Paulo, Brazil, 1985. Her group shows include the Museum of Modern Art, New York; and the Universitario del Choppo, Mexico City. She has co-currated several exhibits including *Latin American Women Artists Living in New York; Choice Works; Connections Project/Conexus*. She is the founder of the *Latin American Women Artists Series* in New York City where she has lived since 1976.

"I work with a Diary of Images, an on-going process that records stories, events, memories, fantasies...The perception of women is the veil that permeates the different layers of reality. I use the photographic camera as an information-gathering tool. Silkscreen multiplies these images. The works represented here are part of a new series *Diary of Images: She is visited by birds and turtles*. This new work is about finding a statehood within myself. It is about carrying history within the shapes of my own turtle shell. It is the fantasy of flight. It is the realization that the turtle carries her own shell through waters and savannahs."